MATA AUSTRONESIA

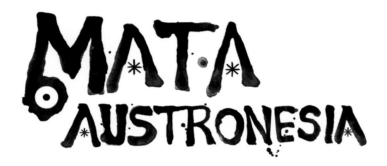

MATA AUSTRONESIA

STORIES FROM AN OCEAN WORLD

AN (ETHNO)GRAPHIC NOVEL

TUKI DRAKE

UNIVERSITY OF HAWAI'I PRESS

HONOLULU

First printing, 2022

Library of Congress Cataloging-in-Publication Data

Names: Drake, Tuki, author, illustrator.
Title: Mata Austronesia : stories from an ocean world / Tuki Drake.
Description: Honolulu : University of Hawai'i Press, 2022. | "An
  (ethno)graphic novel." | Includes bibliographical references. |
  Audience: Grades 10-12 | Audience: 14 years and up
Identifiers: LCCN 2021050470 | ISBN 9780824884567 (trade paperback) | ISBN
  9780824893323 (adobe pdf)
Subjects: LCSH: Pacific Islanders—Juvenile fiction. | Pacific
  Islanders—Comic books, strips, etc. | Islands of the Pacific—Juvenile
  fiction. | Islands of the Pacific—Comic books, strips, etc. | LCGFT:
  Graphic novels.
Classification: LCC PZ7.7.D75 Mat 2022 | DDC 741.5/973—dc23/eng/20211203
LC record available at https://lccn.loc.gov/2021050470

University of Hawai'i Press books are printed on acid-free paper and meet the
guidelines for permanence and durability of the Council on Library Resources.

This book is dedicated to my father and hero,
George Dennis Drake, and to my children, Koa and Tiare.
To know and to love our culture and history.

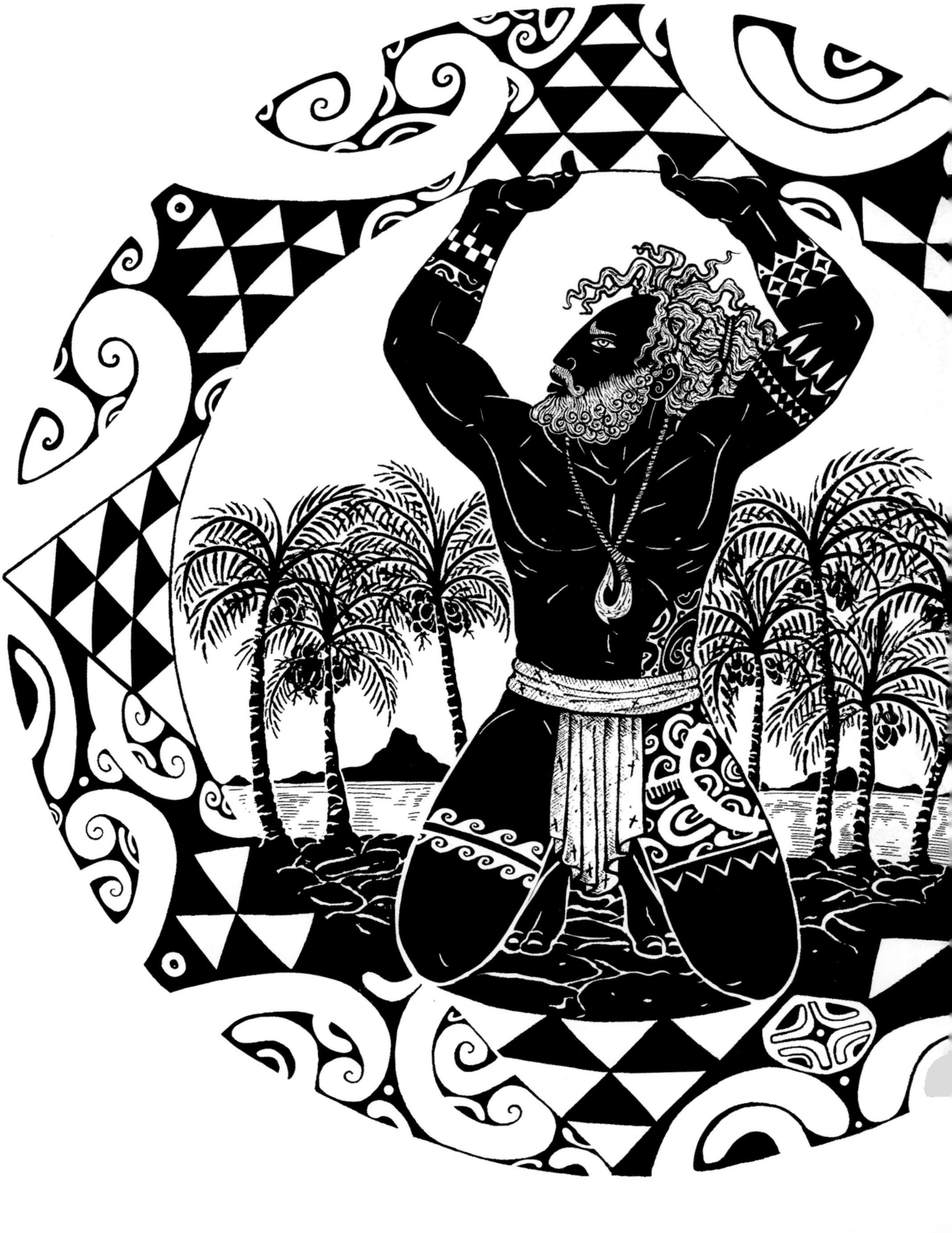

Contents

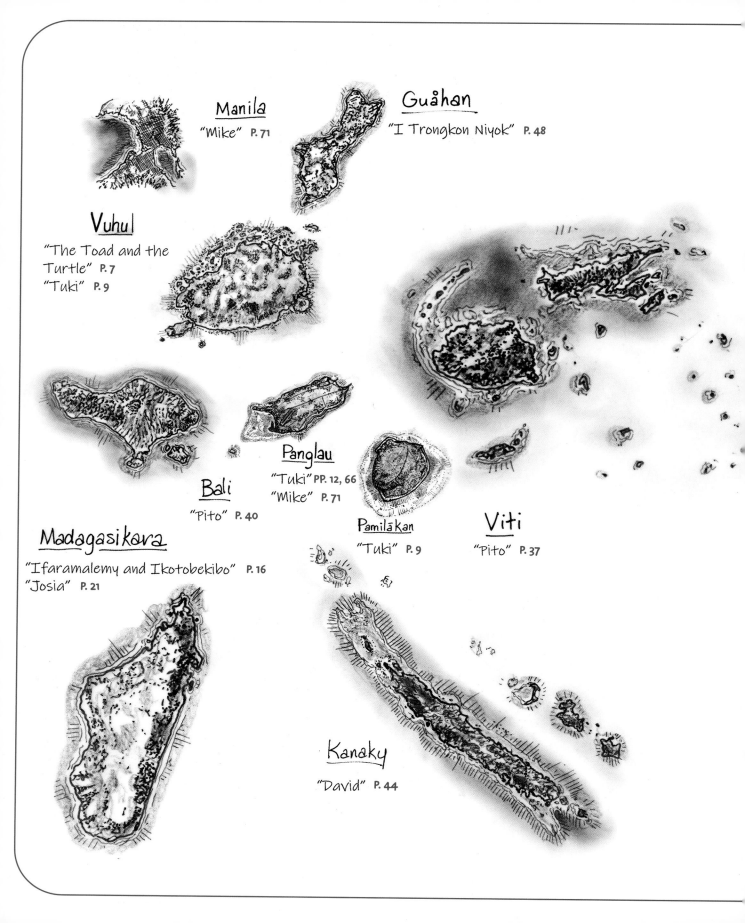

Manila
"Mike" P. 71

Guåhan
"I Trongkon Niyok" P. 48

Vuhul
"The Toad and the
Turtle" P. 7
"Tuki" P. 9

Bali
"Pito" P. 40

Panglau
"Tuki" PP. 12, 66
"Mike" P. 71

Pamilåkan
"Tuki" P. 9

Viti
"Pito" P. 37

Madagasikara
"Ifaramalemy and Ikotobekibo" P. 16
"Josia" P. 21

Kanaky
"David" P. 44

Kaua'i
"Tuki" P. 14

Seattle
"Tuki" P. 13

Arkansas
"Mike" P. 70

Banaba
"Viata" P. 34

O'ahu
"Mike" P. 67

Los Alamitos
"Mike" P. 70

Kiritimati
"Viata" P. 35

Maui
"Mike" P. 67

Tutuila
"Chantelle" P. 26

Tahiti
"Hina and the Eel" P. 46

Taha'a
"Tihoti" P. 52

Rapa Nui
"Hotu Matu'a" P. 60
"Francisco" P. 63

Aotearoa
"Pito" P. 42

Mahalo Nui Ke Akua. Mahalo i Ku'u 'Ohana.

Thanks to my wife, Ashley, and children
For your love and support.
Thanks to my parents...
For always believing in me
Thanks to my Brother and cousin...
For your encouragement.

Mahalo Nui to Dr. Alexander Mawyer

For your ideas, support, encouragement, and
mentorship.
and
Thank you to my editor Emma Ching,
Dr. Terence Wesley-Smith and Dr. Tarcisius Kabutaulaka

Mahalo to My friends for your stories...
This book would be impossible without you!

Mahalo Austronesia and to
the many amazing people that call this
place (places) home.
You are my inspiration.

x

Introduction:

Somewhere in the middle of seeing my mother's life weaken and my first book actually materialize I came to the realization that I had become a very odd sort of historian. I had come to believe that the stories and epics that I knew were important not because they represented people and events whose existence and occurrences could be verified, but because they were lessons to me, and to anyone who cared to listen, about who we are and how we should live our lives. I teach and I write moʻolelo—not history, perhaps as you all know it. I tell stories.

—DR. JONATHAN KAY KAMAKAWIWOʻOLE OSORIO, 2014, P. 14

Our planet, Earth, or more appropriately to my place here in Hawaiʻi nei as I write this, Ka Honua, could fit inside the breadth and width of the Sun, Ka Lā, a thousandfold. Within our galaxy, the star, Betelgeuse, is approximately a thousand times the size of Ka Lā, while the star, VY Canis Majoris, is two thousand times the diameter of Ka Lā. Our solar system, which expands outward 93 million miles, lies within our galaxy, the Milky Way, which stretches 100,000 light-years across and contains more than 100 billion stars and billions more planets. Beyond our galaxy are trillions of other galaxies, billions of light-years apart, existing within an ever-expanding universe churning with innumerable black holes set amidst a canvas rife with immeasurable mysteries. There are more stars in space than grains of sand on Ka Honua. Over 7 billion humans live on the surface of our precious homeworld, each composed of some 37.2 trillion cells fashioned from nearly 2 trillion molecules with every molecule constructed of numerous atoms, which in turn are built up of myriad subatomic particles. All of this rests on the foundations of a quantum realm characterized by unorthodox rules and behaviors that confound our understandings of the palpable world. So, what is the point? Did I just waste the last thirty seconds of your life on this dizzying perspective? Perhaps, but truth be told,

we live on a thin film betwixt two infinitum, macro and micro, wherein all that is or has ever happened, exists. All our stories, our histories, emerge and find their significance within this narrow domain.

There is an *ʻōlelo noʻeau* that says, "*I ka ʻōlelo nō ke ola, i ka ʻōlelo nō ka make*," in words there is life and in words there is death (Pukui, 1983). In some sense, this narrow human domain is another infinity. Within it the histories of individuals and communities are retained in the storyteller's voice, passed on generation after generation, stretching back into pasts so deep as to be times of Creation. Humanity's capacity for oral history, story, and tradition is among its defining attributes, encapsulating the hopes, dreams, wisdom, and knowledge of the ancestors without whom we would not be. As we watch nature buckle under the strain of unchecked and unsustainable human consumption, as our seas' rich marine resources are quickly depleted and replaced by toxic plastic, as storms strengthen and continue to erode our shorelines, the accumulated wisdom embedded in our seafaring ancestors' stories, cultures, and traditions offers profoundly needed insights on how to live in balance with our finite ocean and island resources. Today, such guidance appears ever more crucial to safekeeping not only our local but our planetary future.

Yet, the dominations of Western epistemology in the wake of global colonial incursions by European powers has relegated much of our histories to a space of hearsay, prehistory, or mythology fraught with fiction and amassed as fairy tales. Well-known Pacific historian, David Hanlon (2017) acknowledged this issue when he wrote, "what is known about Oceania's deeper past is for many of us not enough to escape the bonds of prehistory, a designation based on the division of indigenous pasts into the before and after periods of contact with the Euro-American world" (p. 294). For many Indigenous peoples this includes all oral history before (and sometimes after) the arrival of Europeans to their shorelines—thousands of years overshadowed and too often erased by foreign practices, beliefs, values, and ways of thinking in and about the world. Hanlon, in addressing this problem, goes on to say that he would "urge Pacific and World historians to be more tolerant, appreciative, and accommodating of the indigenous histories of Oceania that engage with the deeper past; that are bold, imaginative, and liberating in their approach; that look beyond the conventional lenses of contact, encounter, and colonization; and that embrace varied and distinctive ways of narrating, understanding, and conceptualizing the past" (2017, p. 306). For those of us rooted in Indigenous, Oceanic worlds, the Western invalidation of our deep histories is utterly troublesome, but also presents to us a unique opportunity to raise Austronesian stories and the tradition of storytelling from the mire of irrelevance that outside voices have relegated them to, lifting them up to their proper place amidst the tools of formal history.

Greg Dening's (1991) proposal of a "poetic of histories" that incorporates alternative forms of preserving historical knowledge through "reminiscence, gossip, anecdote, rumour, parable, report, tradition, myth . . . saga, legend, epic, ballad, folklore, annal, chronicle" (pp. 348–349) is a premise for this book. As Australian historian, Chris Ballard (2014) has said of such forms of remembrance, "these are histories that are profoundly performative—they exist in the present and are remade in the act of their communication. They are the praxis of historically and culturally specific forms of historical consciousness, each with their own grammars of expression and criteria of objectivity" (pp. 96–97). This incorporation of "other modes of historical consciousness" (Ballard, 2014, p. 112) opens the door to alternative vantage points for perceiving and understanding the past and its manifold relationships to the present. This book endeavors to reassemble diverse regional voices to reflect Indigenous historicities such as those encoded in myths and legends as it expresses both ancient and modern Austronesian stories on a common plane of relevance. This assemblage of stories bridges related communities of people over vast Oceanic spaces and demonstrates how storytelling is a culturally grounded and invaluable tool for historical transmission, generatively employed by Austronesian Peoples for their families and communities.

Renowned Tongan anthropologist, Epeli Hauʻofa (2008) once wrote that "all social realities are human creations and that if we fail to construct our own realities other people will do it for us." He continued, "I believe that in order for us to gain greater autonomy than we have today and maintain it within the global system, we must in addition to other measures be able to define and construct our pasts and present in our own ways" (p. 60). The purpose for this book is therefore twofold: to elevate and reimagine Austronesian histories through the stories and traditions so knowledgeably crafted and dutifully perpetuated by the Austronesian People over millennia through word of mouth; and, second, to illustrate the interconnectedness of Austronesia as both a diverse and distinct cultural, linguistic, and historical region.

What Is Austronesia?

According to Pacific scholar, David Gegeo, "We need once and for all to eliminate the Anglo-European categories that still tend to imprison us in outdated, meaningless terminologies that divide us rather than unite us, as well as determine our discursive practices. . . . These category labels come with a host of assumptions that are deeply embedded in colonization. . . . Certainly it is easy to get rid of Melanesia, Micronesia, and Polynesia, and refer to people by their islands, that is, by place and space" (2001, p. 179). The geographical fragmentation and colonial and postcolonial reconstitution of Austronesian places within arbitrary regional imaginations, that is, Madagascar (Madagasikara) into Africa, the Indonesian, Malaysian, and Philippine Islands into Asia, and the demarcating of Pacific places into the categories of Micronesia, Melanesia, and Polynesia, was not only a passing scholarly or geopolitical act. Rather, it was one that impacted Indigenous identity and lived experience. Gegeo (2001) conjectures that referring "to people by their islands" is one, more Pacific, way to rearticulate regional divisions; however, he also mentions the need to "develop a new vocabulary" that does not "imprison us in outdated, meaningless terminologies" (p. 179). Epeli Hauʻofa's (1994) wave-making idea of an inclusive Oceania for both Native and "adopted" (p. 155), "a regional identity anchored in our common heritage of the ocean" that "transcend[s] all forms of insularity, to become one that is openly searching, inventive, and welcoming" like the sea (Hauʻofa, 2008b, p. 40), does much to "unite us" (Gegeo, 2001, p. 179). Nevertheless, even Hauʻofa's grand vision seems nearsighted when he writes "that Pacific Ocean islands from Japan, through the Philippines and Indonesia, which are adjacent to the Asian mainland, do not have oceanic cultures, and are therefore not part of Oceania" (Hauʻofa, 2008b, p. 38). Hauʻofa (2008b) goes on to indicate that he is indignant over being "lumped together with hundreds of millions of Asians," which he signals as "progressive marginalization" (pp. 45–46), but what about the homogenization of the countless diverse peoples that inhabit the vast Asian continent and its nearshore islands as delineated by Western powers of cartography? Would Hauʻofa consider them a monolith? Does the Pacific Ocean only touch the shores of the islands of Palau and Papua New Guinea and bypass those of Maluku, Kepulauan Ayu, Timor-Leste, Sulawesi, Mindanao, and Bali?

In her 2017 book *Becoming Landowners: Entanglements of Custom and Modernity in Papua New Guinea and Timor-Leste*, Victoria Stead struggles with these arbitrary distinctions when she writes that "Papua New Guinea and Timor-Leste (are) two Pacific Island countries whose histories, cultures, and politics both resonate with and diverge from one another in engaging ways. Both countries are, broadly speaking, Melanesian, with Papua New Guinea very firmly so and Timor-Leste sitting more ambivalently on the cusp of Melanesia and Asia" (p. 5). On Western maps, political and geographical regions are clearly defined with pen and ink, which ignores the reality that, like water, peoples flow between and through each other as they have done for eons.

Reflecting on relationships between geographical imaginaries and the politics of lived experience, Edward Said (1978), a noted Palestinian-American scholar and philosopher, wrote that "there are Westerners, and there are Orientals. The former dominate; the latter must be dominated, which usually means having their land occupied, their internal affairs rigidly controlled, their blood and treasure put at the disposal of one or another Western power" (p. 36). The regional label was utilized to divide men "into 'us' (Westerners) and 'they' (Orientals)" (Said, 1978, p. 45), Said went on to note that "Asia speaks through and by virtue of the European imagination, which is depicted as victorious over Asia, that hostile 'other' world beyond the seas. To Asia are given the feelings of emptiness, loss, and disaster that seem thereafter to reward Oriental challenges to the West; and also, the lament that in some glorious past Asia fared better" (p. 56). Orientalism is Pan-Asianism, idealizing a closed system of similar languages, beliefs, ethnicities, histories, and cultures, while promoting the fiction that Asians "almost everywhere (are) nearly the same" (Said, 1978, p. 38). Asia's geographic boundaries extend from Turkey in the west to Japan in the east, from Russia in the north to Indonesia and Timor-Leste in the south—the largest continent on the planet and its most diverse in terms of cultures, languages, and ethnicities. Asia has nevertheless become a geographic invention of the West, at once incorrectly implying homogeneity where there is none (Şengör et al., 2019), while simultaneously erasing other profound ties and relationships—as with the Austronesian islands of "Southeast Asia" and Oceania.

Austronesians

As Emerson Odango (2015), a diasporic Filipino scholar, writes in the article "Austronesian Youth Perspectives on Language Reclamation and Maintenance": "I find support not only in

Indeed, a strong case could be made for extending Oceania at least to Taiwan, the homeland of the Austronesian language family whose speakers colonised significant parts of the region from about 6,000 years ago. Recuperation of the original, broad scope of Oceania is justified on several grounds. Pragmatically, it redresses the heavy Polynesian emphasis in much recent literature on European voyages and encounters with Pacific Islanders; and it flouts modern geopolitics while not discounting strategic postcolonial usages which restrict Oceania to the Pacific Islands and perhaps Australasia. Historically, the (re)expansion of Oceania admits ancient, far-flung affinities of origin, language, customs and material culture, as well as critical human trajectories in the region over 40–60 millennia (including those of Europeans after 1511), until the freezing of colonial borders in the late 19th century. Politically, an inclusive notion of Oceania problematises the hyper-realism of the modern states which inherited those colonial borders, leaving a shrunken Oceania severed from Island Southeast Asia; the island of New Guinea truncated; Bougainville separated from Solomon Islands; and Australia poised uneasily on the margins of both Asia and the Island Pacific. Academically, it challenges the conventional division of labour in the disciplines of history, politics, international relations, economics, geography and anthropology, which mutually quarantine Asian, Australian and Pacific Studies though archaeology and prehistoric linguistics are honourable exceptions to this rule.

—BRONWEN DOUGLAS, 2010, PP. 1–2

the fact that (Austronesians) share similar experiences in the formation of our linguistic identities but also in my realization that we are connected by language and culture to a shared Austronesian ancestry" (p. 98). He adds that "I find great inspiration in being able to look back at my linguistic genealogy as an Austronesian person because it allows me to contextualize my experiences . . . with those of my generational cohort who come from places such as Taiwan, the Philippines, East Timor, Palau, the Mortlocks, Pohnpei, Kiribati, Fiji, Aotearoa, and Hawaiʻi" (p. 100). If we must have regions, superimposed demarcations of inclusivity and exclusivity over land and sea, what might it mean to the Indigenous peoples and local communities to eliminate the (post)colonial regional identities, adopt the spirit of Hauʻofa's Oceania sans ethnocentrism (Wesley-Smith, 1995, p. 125) and expand it with a *vision of Austronesia,* to cover the entire breadth of the ethnolinguistic and cultural influence region that includes Madagascar (Madagasikara), the Comoros, Maritime Southeast Asia, Micronesia, Polynesia, and much of Melanesia?

As both an Austronesian and a descendant of English mariners, I find the history of European sea exploration and mapmaking both fascinating and enraging. The term Polynésie was first employed in Europe in the second half of the 1700s and "encompassed 'everything in the vast Pacific Ocean'" (Douglas, 2010, pp. 196–197). Océanique was coined in 1804 by the French geographers "Edme Mentelle and Conrad Malte-Brun," but the term was eventually truncated to Océanie and the region institutionally reified, divided, and codified by "navigator-naturalist" Jules-Sébastien-César Dumont d'Urville "into four 'principal divisions': Polynésie, Micronésie ('Micronesia'), Malaisie ('Malaysia') and Mélanésie ('Melanesia') which included Australie ('Australia')" (Douglas, 2010, p. 197). Our contemporary "tripartite division" of the Pacific resulted from this outside process and has subsequently been generationally ingrained and adopted by Pacific Islanders though it lacks "biological and cultural" substance (Spriggs, 2009, p. 10). Tarcisius Kabutaulaka (2015) writes that "this was not just a geographical mapping of the region; it was also a racialist mapping that reflected long-held ideas about race and social evolution (in Europe)" (p. 111). The consequences of this imported "ethnological typology" is continued subversion of "indigenous genealogical plots of connection and difference across the Pacific," according to Margaret Jolly (2007, pp. 515–516). Stephen Winduo (2000), speaking to the cartographic powers of Western imperialists and responding to the thoughts of author Simon Ryan, writes, "Ryan explains that erasure and cartographic practices overwhelmingly legitimated 'the erasure of existing social and geo-cultural formations in preparation for the projection and subsequent emplacement of a new order.' The exercise of power is immediately deployed in order that control

is exercised, legitimated, and instituted as a geopolitical and cultural entity." Ryan sees in this exercise a "cartographic double movement, or erasure and projection, creating a blank, and filling that blank with a legend (both in the sense of a myth and a cartographical inscription) [that] continued into the eighteenth century'" (pp. 599–600).

The first "blind crossing" in the Pacific, a term employed by Matthew Spriggs (2009) to indicate journeys across seas wherein the sight of all land is lost, was accomplished 26,000 years ago by the forebearers of "indigenous New Guineans and Australian Aboriginals" when they left the Sahul continent to go to the Manus Islands (pp. 10–11). They were the earliest known inhabitants of Oceania. Then, approximately 6,000 years ago, the proto-Austronesians migrated across the sea to Taiwan (Kun, 2007, pp. 92–93). They proved to be capable seafarers and came to inhabit and develop a maritime cultural hearth in what is now classified as "Island Southeast Asia" leading to "the next blind crossings in the Pacific" approximately 3,000 years ago (Spriggs, 2009, p. 11), with a branch moving east into "Micronesia," another west to Madagascar, and yet another continuing down, southeast, into the "Melanesian" Islands (Finney, 2007, pp. 106, 133). The latter group traveled through Vanuatu and on to Fiji, then Tonga and Samoa, eventually colonizing the rest of the easternmost Pacific archipelagos like the Marquesas, Hawaiʻi, Tahiti, Mangareva, and as far south as Aotearoa, New Zealand (Finney, 2007, p. 135). The culture of these first Austronesians who ventured into the remote Pacific is called Lapita, "being named after an archeological site in New Caledonia" (Spriggs, 2009, p. 11), and is "itself . . . to some extent a hybrid of Island Southeast Asian and the earlier cultures of Continental and Island Melanesia" (p. 20). According to Patrick Kirch, celebrated professor of archeology now at the University of Hawaiʻi at Mānoa, "the distinctive Lapita pottery establishes these sites as having been occupied by closely related groups of people, sharing a common set of artistic rules and conventions, as are only found within a single culture" (2000, p. 91). He adds that "the pottery excavated from the earliest Lapita sites in the Bismarck archipelago is undeniably related to the ceramics from contemporary or slightly older sites in Halmahera, Talaud, Sulawesi, and the Philippines (p. 93). Within "8–10 generations," Austronesians bringing their Lapita culture, had successfully explored and settled most of the Pacific (Spriggs, 2009, p. 11) thousands of years before the first Europeans discovered it (Jolly, 2007, p. 514). Vicente "Vince" Diaz (2011) reflecting on this astounding feat by his Austronesian ancestors, wrote that much like linguistic cognates—such as the word for sky, *langit,* which occurs in slight variations from Madagascar all the way to Hawaiʻi—the outrigger canoe and its variations are material cognates reflective of a shared ancestral archetype (p. 23).

Recent genetic evidence dismisses the notion of a large unrelated mass of peoples entering the Pacific through the Philippines from Taiwan (Penny and Meyer, 2007, pp. 98–99). A 2016 study by Pontus Skoglund and colleagues that conducted DNA analysis on the skeletal remains of four Lapita-aged women in Vanuatu and Tonga, revealed that the original Austronesian Lapita settlers of Near and Remote Oceania, some 3,000 years ago, shared "all their ancestry with the indigenous Atayal people in Taiwan and the Kankanaey people in the Philippines" (Gibbons 2016). Quite aside from rapidly evolving genetics research, it is apparent that Austronesians share striking commonalities in language, tradition, culture, and even cuisine (Bellwood, Fox, and Tryon, 1995, p. 3; Irwin, 2007, pp. 67–69). In the past, such similarities have been attributed as coincidental adoptions by preexisting peoples located in comparable environments through cross-cultural exchange or enculturation. Granting that much of this did go on, Bellwood, Fox, and Tryon (1995) argue that,

> one must surely reject any explanation for the Austronesian languages that would see them as spread ancestrally by borrowing or by convergence amongst static pre-existing populations. In other words, unmoving peoples, already highly diversified, did not simply "borrow" Austronesian languages from one another . . . the whole picture makes sense, and obviously so for the far-flung islands of the Pacific and Madagascar, if one accepts that the ancestral versions of the modern Austronesian languages were spread mainly by colonizing speakers . . . on a whole-language-family scale with both great extent and time-depth, no other explanation apart from spread by colonization makes sense. (pp. 2–3)

It is also apparent that early Austronesians expanded outward rapidly from their home islands in Southeast Asia to settle the plethora of islands in the Pacific and Indian Oceans bringing with them their unique language, culture, traditions, beliefs, plants, animals, and maritime innovations that evolved, diversified, and specialized over time (Finney, 2007, pp. 135–137). Genetic, archeological, linguistic, and anthropological research all support an inclusive and expansive reinterpretation of the Austronesian ethnolinguistic region removed from the anachronistic, largely unsubstantiated and colonially contrived Western partitions and designations that have left the region divided, truncated, and diminished. This evidence-supported vision for Austronesia emboldens new interdisciplinary pedagogies and challenges preconceived Oceanic hierarchies while reaffirming ancestral linkages. It binds together scattered chapters to reveal a larger, more comprehensive familial story, a story already embedded in the languages and oral traditions of all Austronesians.

On Language

Language is one important key to our histories. It unlocks pathways between distant places and traverses millennia in an instant. The multitude of Austronesian languages reveals our interconnected histories while reasserting our diversity and complexity. However, our Austronesian languages, like our geographies, have been reinterpreted by the West and it is critical for us to reexamine the ways in which colonization and globalization have affected them.

I hope this work encourages the reader to become aware of and reflect upon the codification of non-Western Austronesian languages using a Western alphabet as a form of continued colonization that simplifies and standardizes language diversity for the ease of Western forms of reading and writing. This is a process of erasure and substitution that creates a false narrative of linguistic homogeneity based on geographic proximity. When this narrative is passed on to future generations of Native and non-Native speakers it effectively discredits alternative pronunciations without allowing Indigenous and Native speakers to question the validity of the standardized Western spellings assigned to their own words. I am pushing back against this subtle form of cultural theft.

I am a Native of Bohol on my mother's side and have spent countless hours discussing with fellow Bol-anons on how the spelling of Bol-anon words has continued to evolve since the arrival of the Latin alphabet to our shores. I contend that in many varieties of spoken Bol-anon, a Central Visayan language closely related to Cebuano, the /v/ and the /b/ sounds are not separate, clearly defined phonemes as in English; rather, the Visayan /b/ is perhaps best understood as a soft /b/ that can approximate a voiced bilabial fricative /β/. This explains the use of both /v/ and /b/ in the terms "Visayan" and "Bisayan." Regarding the arbitrary nature of Visayan orthography, many Bol-anon words now being spelled with a /k/ were once spelled with a /c/. The /c/ and the /k/ were largely interchangeable depending on preference such as seen in "banca" or "bangka," referring to an outrigger canoe. Likewise, John U. Wolff's *A Dictionary of Cebuano Visayan* published in 1972 only utilized the vowels /a/, /i/, and /u/, wherein now the vowels /e/ and /o/ have been added and are commonly employed but can also be rightly pronounced as /i/ or /u/ depending on speaker preference. For instance, the word for breadfruit is now spelled "kulo" but pronounced, "kulu." There is no tangible difference between the /u/ and the /o/.

In *Relacion de las Yslas Filipinas* written in 1582 by the Spanish conquistador Miguel de Loarca, the island of Bohol is repeatedly referred to as "Vohol." In one instance, Loarca mentions both "Butuan" and "Vohol" in the same sentence, both of which are now spelled with the letter /b/. Firstly, this illustrates the innate instability and lack of distinction between the /b/ and /v/ sound in the Spanish language and secondly it implies a similar lack of distinction in Bol-anon and other closely related Visayan languages.

I have chosen to use John U. Wolff's *A Dictionary of Cebuano Visayan* along with standard Hawaiian orthography as models to inform how I write the Bol-anon words for this book. The vowels therefore are: /a/, /i/, and /u/ while the consonants are /'/ (glottal stop), /d/, /g/, /h/, /j/, /k/, /l/, /m/, /n/, /ng/, /p/, /r/, /s/, /t/, /v/, and /w/. The /v/ is still pronounced as a standard Visayan /b/, which is to say a soft /b/, possible /β/. The 'okina and the kahakō are two innovations from 'Ōlelo Hawai'i that I strongly feel should be incorporated into Bol-anon orthography. The kahakō represented by "‾" when used in this context symbolizes the elongation and/or stress of a particular vowel. The 'okina represented by " ' " denotes a glottal stop as in the English, "uh-oh."

The following are examples of this system in use with the current spelling of the words listed first followed by my revised spelling: "Bisayan" and "Binisaya" becomes "Visaian" and "Vinisaia"; "Dao," "Baclayon," and "Panglao" (place-names) become "Da'u"; "Vaklaiun," and "Panglau"; "Looc" and "Loon" (place-names) become "Lū'uk" and "Lū'un"; "maajo nga hapon" (good afternoon) becomes "ma'āju nga hāpun"; "banca/bangka" (canoe) becomes "vanka"/ "vangka"; "iro"/ "ido" (dog) becomes "iru"/ "idu"; "ako" (I) becomes "aku"; while "oo"/"o" (agree) becomes "'ū'u" and "'ū."

My taking liberty with the spelling of the Bol-anon language may offend and upset some fellow Bol-anons and for that I am sorry. Linguist Kenneth L. Rehg writes, "Don't rush into the task of creating or revising an alphabet until you are confident you understand the phonology of the language. Faulty phonological analyses give rise to faulty orthographies" (2004, p. 506). In heading Regh's warning, it is important to note that I am not a linguist; and, although, I am ethnically Bol-anon of mixed heritage and was born and raised on Bohol as a young child, I moved away quite early on while continuing to make frequent pilgrimages back to Bohol to maintain my connection. I have since largely gravitated toward using English and 'Ōlelo Hawai'i due to having spent a large part of my life in places and around people who use these languages. I am still in the process of reclaiming my ancestral tongue; therefore, this respelling, or reimagining of Bol-anon orthography, is not prescriptive, as it is certainly flawed, but rather my effort to ask the reader, particularly Bol-anon (Vul'anun) and Austronesian readers, to reevaluate the ways in which the imported Latin alphabet, colonization, and even academia have been reframing their native tongue, and to encourage them to question and actively incorporate any of the orthographical changes they would like to see in how their language is spelled and even pronounced. I am asking

Native and Indigenous Austronesians to reclaim authority over their ancestral tongues. Ultimately, perhaps a non-Latin-based orthography, like Baybayin, is the ideal when writing Austronesian languages and that is a discussion that should happen as well. In this same spirit, the spelling of some words from the various Austronesian languages within the stories found in this book were chosen by the individual storyteller and may differ from their standardized form.

Mata Austronesia

I have chosen storytelling as a vehicle to illuminate these Austronesian connections because, like Dr. Osorio, I consider myself a kind of storyteller. Amongst the numerous Austronesian languages, the many cognates for the word "eye," *mata*, remain relatively unchanged from one another despite the vast oceanic distances and time separating the various Austronesian peoples. *Mata*, therefore, symbolizes and embodies the shared heritage, ancestral memory, and cultural legacy of Austronesia as a diverse yet distinct ethnolinguistic region spread across an immense saltwater realm. It also figuratively represents the reader being given a vision, a visually interesting glimpse, into the many worlds presented by the Austronesian storytellers in this work. This is an (ethno)graphic novel, a collection of illustrated stories told from the perspective of the people from the region created to engage readers outside of academia with interconnected tales from the Austronesian past and present. There are ten parts, fourteen chapters, one historical migration map, and an illustrated appendix that comprise this (ethno)graphic novel. Each part is about a specific Austronesian place or regionally and culturally significant topic. There are eight personal accounts, life stories, short anecdotes in this book that were shared by storytellers, my friends, from the region with one account being my own. These stories reflect what is most important to the storyteller about their home, culture, life, or issues that they want to address. In addition, there are five ancestral stories, oral traditions, two of which pertain to the creation and founding of an island, specifically Vuhul (Bohol) in part I and Rapa Nui in part IX, one which speaks to food traditions in Madagasikara (Madagascar) found in part II, and two others in part VII that address the origins of the coconut tree in Tahiti and Guåhan, an invaluable plant to many Austronesian societies. Part V is unique in that it contains descriptions of afterbirth terms and practices from Bali, Vuhul (Bohol), Viti (Fiji), and Aotearoa (New Zealand). The illustrated appendix at the end of the book includes a brief compendium of visualized linguistic cognates from several Austronesian languages. Ultimately, this book was a labor of love and relied solely on the generous story contributions of my friends who together represent only a very few select islands, languages, and cultures out of the many thousands found within Austronesia. Readers should therefore view this book as a brief glimpse of the region, an invitation for deeper study, and an introduction to the numerous academic disciplines that explore the many facets of this extraordinarily diverse, captivating, and engaging place.

This work dreams of building upon the noble foundations of Epeli Hau'ofa's vision of Oceania in order to expand its reach toward ever necessary reclamation of Indigenous identity and all of the politics of the everyday lived experiences across this extraordinary region. Hau'ofa (2008b) noted that "our ancestors wrote our histories on the landscape and the seascape; carved, stencilled and wove our metaphors on objects of utility; and sang and danced in rituals and ceremonies for the propitiation of the awesome forces of nature and society" (p. 40). Reimagining an Austronesian identity based on shared history, language, and culture while unyoking it from disingenuous and fictitious colonial frameworks in order to foster greater regional understanding and mutual respect is a worthwhile scholarly pursuit. However, in order to better understand the "prehistoric," deep-time interconnections and entanglements of our Austronesian predecessors, we must shift away from regionally biased research methodologies and embrace a more holistic approach to research and data that incorporates multiple historicities (Ballard, 2014, p. 113) and epistemologies (Subramani, 2001, p. 151). Colonization succeeded and continues to use the process of erasure, replacement, and acquiescence to survive. Matthew Spriggs (2009) writes that "wider knowledge of an ancient shared history between the peoples of the Pacific Islands can only be to the good . . . it helps break down the lingering insidiousness of views of racial hierarchy still held by outsiders and internalised by some Pacific Islanders themselves, to

the detriment of all" (p. 21). There is strength in unity and the idea of Austronesia builds on the ethnolinguistic and historical reality of a related people who successfully settled the far corners of both the Indian and Pacific Oceans far before European contact.

Ultimately, this book of stories is for the Austronesian community, the Indigenous peoples and local communities living in the islands and in the diaspora. It was created to give fresh voice to peoples of Austronesian descent, and to our friends and colleagues of all heritages, by producing an engaging platform to share stories that meaningfully summon our broad and deeply shared Oceanian world into view. Our tapestry of stories, traditions, and cultures formed over thousands of years prospering in an Ocean world contains unique, vital, pragmatic, and contemporarily applicable wisdom on living within our planet's limited natural means. Mo'olelo—stories—contextualize the staggering immensity of the cosmos and impart meaning to visible and invisible realms. Our stories permeate the fabric of our being. Through storytellers our past and present are interwoven and preserved within our narrow human domain. This work is not advocating the uniformity of Austronesian Peoples. On the contrary, it is intended to showcase the multiplicity of identities, histories, ethnicities, cultures, languages, and storytelling traditions among people of Austronesian descent. Austronesians are not culturally or historically monolithic; yet, despite our many differences, we do share common ancestry. It is this shared ancestry that unites us and is the focus of this book. My hope is that this work helps open fresh avenues of conversation and connections between Austronesian communities both unified and long separated by oceans of time and space, and by deeply embedded Western colonial and cartographic intrusions.

MATA
AUSTRONESIA

Part 1:
My Heart Is an
Austronesian Canoe

Connecting Places and People

Austronesians have shared ancestry originating somewhere in ancient coastal southern China. Approximately 6,000 years ago, these Proto-Austronesian speakers migrated from continental Asia across the sea to Taiwan. Around 2200–2500 BC, they crossed the Bashi Channel into the islands of the "Philippine" archipelago. These early Austronesians were exceptionally skilled seafarers and developed a unique maritime culture in the islands of "Southeast Asia." Between 1600 BC and 1 AD, Austronesians pushed farther southeast through "Melanesia."

These Austronesians were known for their distinctive style of pottery, first noted by archeologists at a site called "Lapita" in Kanaky. Henceforth known as Lapita people, they were the forebears of many in the Pacific. These original Lapita settlers spread rapidly from Island Southeast Asia to Near Oceania, and then swiftly onward into Remote Oceania.

AUSTRONESIAN MIGRATION MAP

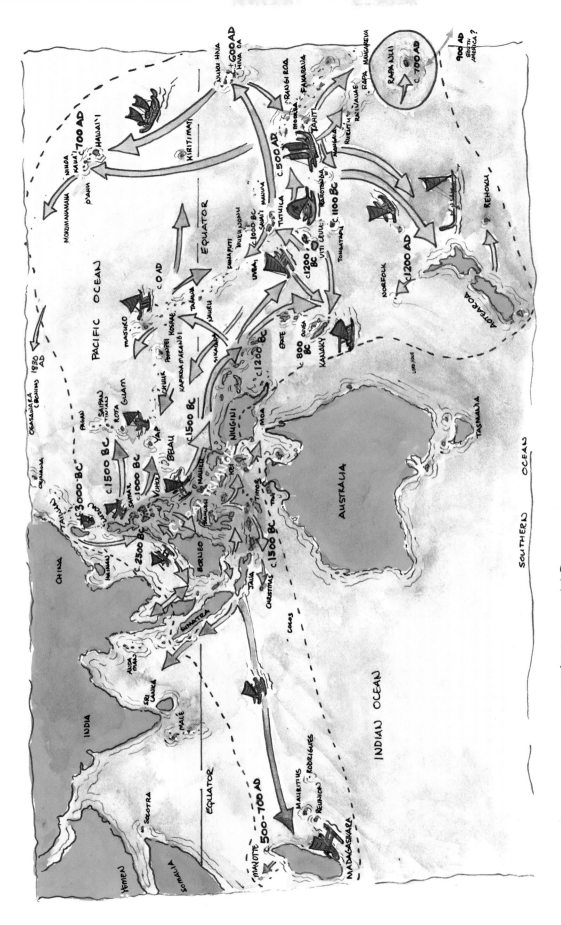

This map models Austronesian migration history through Maritime Southeast Asia, the Indian and Pacific Oceans. The dates and directional arrows serve as approximations of initial Austronesian settlement periods based on scholarly research in a variety of interrelated fields with available and evolving data. The reality is, these migrations were complex individual stories involving countless individual stories taking place over thousands of years, with Austronesians maintaining travel and trade routes across vast expanses of ocean for millennia. Our Austronesian ancestors were not constrained by Western-imposed colonial boundaries and labels. For the Austronesians, the Ocean was a place of limitless imagination, exploration, and possibilities.

Austronesian explorers were initially a small, relatively uniform, and culturally developed group that managed to spread and diversify across two of the world's largest oceans.

From Madagasikara to Rapa Nui, from the African continent to the Americas, Austronesian-speaking Peoples sailing and paddling aboard their outrigger and double-hulled voyaging canoes have left their indelible mark.

The Toad and the Turtle

Long ago in the ancient past, people lived in the heavens beyond the clouds. All was well, until one day, the only daughter of the high chief, *datu*, fell gravely ill. Many were perplexed as to how to cure her ailment, *sākit*.

The *datu*'s priests and healers, *mananawal*, said that the cure rested in the roots of the great *valīti*, banyan tree.

Together, the *datu* and his men dug a trench around the roots of the great *valīti*. The *datu* laid his daughter in the trench. Her arms needed to touch the roots . . .

. . . for her to be healed!

Unfortunately, they had dug too deep. She fell through a hole in the sky and down past the clouds! Two wandering whistling ducks, *gākit*, swooped up to rescue her. She rested on their backs as they flew.

In those days, there was only an endless ocean, *lāwud*. The two *gākit* found Big Turtle and showed him the unwell woman. Big Turtle, concerned, realized they needed to make her a terrestrial home.

BIG TURTLE, WHAT DO WE DO?

FEAR NOT, MANGA GĀKIT, I HAVE A PLAN!

Big Turtle called together a council of creatures to try and bring up sand from the ocean floor. Many tried, but all failed. Finally, Old Toad volunteered.

I'LL BRING UP THE SAND.

GOOD LUCK.

Old Toad held her breath and kicked powerfully downward until she reached the seafloor.

Old Toad gathered sand in her mouth, ascended, and then heaped it one mouthful at a time onto Big Turtle's colossal shell. She repeated this . . .

Until, finally, due to her steadfast efforts, Big Turtle's shell was transformed into an island suitable for the woman. This is how the island of Vuhul began, on the back of a great turtle.

On the island, the woman married a man and had two sons. One of the sons, Good One, sculpted a male and female out of the soil. He then spit on them, which gave them life. They became the first Vul'anons.

Tuki .

I remember the cold, howling wind and trying to be brave as the waves berated our little *vanka*, Visaian outrigger canoe, which was powered by a small and noisy diesel motor. The creaking wood, the warping bamboo *kātig*, outriggers, flexing under the strain of a violent sea as salt spray mixed with rain, soaking us in a tropical deluge.

My father was taking my brother and me to the *pulo*, island, of Pamilākan. This was my first trip across the sea and it certainly did not disappoint.

My father, as always, was a voice of calm. As we plunged in and out of the tumultuous surf, I held onto his words like a life vest, which we did not have.

DON'T WORRY, THIS IS JUST A "SMALL" STORM, BOYS. THIS *VANKA* HAS BEEN THROUGH MUCH WORSE. IT CAN HANDLE IT.

As we approached Pamilākan's shore, the squall dissipated and gave way to the hot morning sun. Disembarking over the white sand, I exhaled with relief.

WE SURVIVED!

On the north coast of the island, overlooking the beach, stood an old, crumbling Spanish watchtower, a relic from 300 years of European colonization and influence on the Visaian Islands.

A local Pamilākan man then showed us the burial cave of his ancestors. Bodies of the deceased were left to decompose in large tins until only their bones remained. Hundreds of years of ancestral bones were carefully preserved in this sacred space.

Pamilākan is an arid island, supposedly named after the *pamilāk* or *pilāk*, a specialized fishhook for whale sharks, manta rays, and dolphins. The island is a little less than a square mile in land area but surrounded by a life-rich turquoise sea.

A man carrying the carcass of a *sanga*, manta ray, passed us on the only road running across the center of the island.

My father greeted him as we passed. Pamilākans at that time were prolific *sanga* and *tuki tuki* or *valilan*, whale shark, hunters. Tourism has since replaced hunting with conservation and a monetary economy.

The beach on the south end of the island was studded with the sun-bleached bones of gentle sea giants. That evening, we sailed back to Vuhul over much calmer seas.

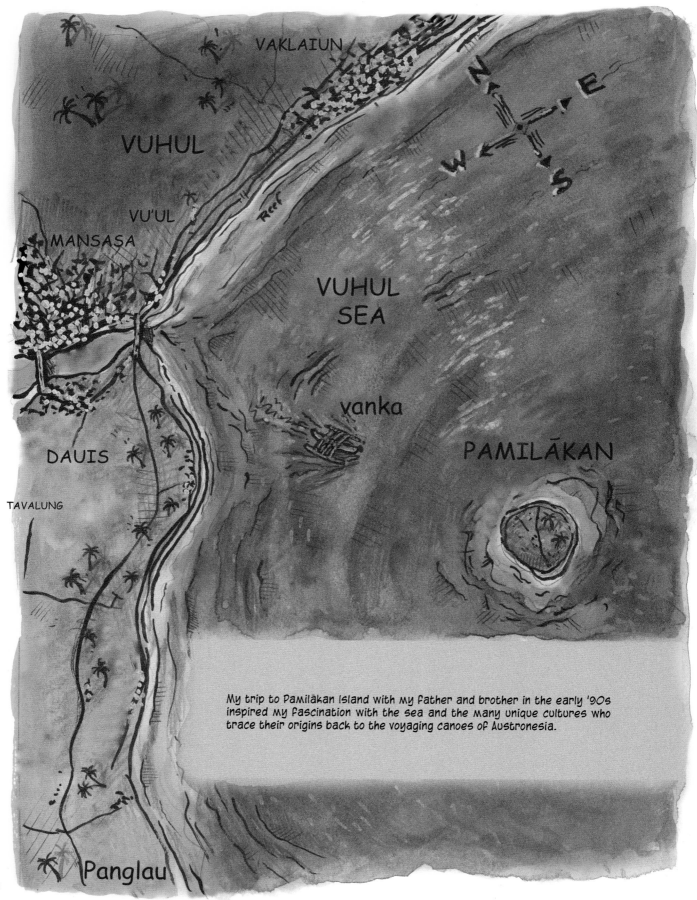

VAKLAIUN

VUHUL

VU'UL

MANSASA

VUHUL
SEA

vanka

PAMILĀKAN

DAUIS

TAVALUNG

My trip to Pamilākan Island with my father and brother in the early '90s inspired my fascination with the sea and the many unique cultures who trace their origins back to the voyaging canoes of Austronesia.

Panglau

By 2010, I had left the islands of the tropical Pacific and worked as a stocker at a large home improvement warehouse in Seattle, Washington. I began my day at 3:30 a.m. walking to work in the slushy snow, occasionally piquing the interest of passing police officers because of my beard and dark complexion.

City life proved to be difficult for me, and the constant cold, rain, and overcast skies compounded my dissatisfaction. I made it one whole year before being drawn back to the islands' warm embrace.

I NEED TO GET A FAUCET IN THIS AISLE! HOW MUCH LONGER?!

MA'AM, I'M SORRY BUT MY ASSOCIATE IS CURRENTLY DOING HIS BEST TO PULL DOWN A 250-POUND WATER HEATER FROM THE TOP SHELF BY HIMSELF. WE'RE GOING TO NEED A COUPLE MORE MINUTES. . . . THANK YOU!

The best part of that job was taking lunch breaks with my coworkers, fellow Islanders, from Guåhan, Luzon, and Madagasikara. We spoke about history, culture, language, and integrating into Seattle city society. We formed a bond through our commonalities rather than differences.

WHAT IS YOUR WORD FOR "EYE"?

MATA

MATA

MÃTA

MASO

Luzon

I AM NOT "ASIAN," I AM LITERALLY AN ISLANDER OF THE PACIFIC OCEAN.

MY PEOPLE SAILED ACROSS THE INDIAN OCEAN MANY MILLENNIA AGO FROM BORNEO.

Madagasikara

Guåhan

IT'S CLEAR. WE ARE ALL RELATED AND WE ARE ALL ISLANDERS.

When I asked them what they identified as, they replied:

I realized from our many conversations that we had all descended from a great seafaring people, joint heirs to an Austronesian heritage, connected across oceans of time and space to common ancestors who navigated to the ends of the earth and back, making their home amongst a Hau'ofan *Sea of Islands*.

By my mid-twenties, I was volunteering on weekends to work on the Nāmāhoe, the *wa'a kaulua*, Hawaiian double-hulled voyaging canoe, of Kaua'i. This two-decade-long project was the brainchild of Hōkūle'a voyagers: John Kruse, Dr. Patrick Aiu, and Dennis Chun.

In my free time, I rebuilt a single-man *wa'a*, Hawaiian outrigger canoe, which I enjoyed paddling and fishing from outside of 'Anini and Hanalei on the island of Kaua'i.

As I watched the tide recede, exposing the colorful coral heads, I thought of my Austronesian ancestors whose lives were so intertwined with their natural environment.

Pacific scholar and writer, Albert Wendt (1983) wrote, "I belong to Oceania—or, at least, I am rooted in a fertile part of it and it nourishes my spirit, helps to define me, and feeds my imagination."

Part II: Malagasy Memories

Ifaramalemy and Ikotobèkibo

A long time ago, on the island of Madagasikara in a little house at the edge of a large forest lived two orphans.

Ikotobekibo and Ifaramalemy were brother and sister. Ifaramalemy was a kind sister who took care of her brother, while Ikotobekibo was selfish and would always eat all their food.

Over the years, Ifaramalemy grew thinner while Ikotobekibo became much fatter.

One day, a famished Ifaramalemy snuck into their neighbor Itrimobé's bountiful garden and stole two ripe bananas and a sweet potato.

She gave the delicious bananas to her brother who then also decided to sneak into Itrimobé's garden.

In the middle of the night, Ikotobekibo started stealing fruits from the garden. He ate until he could not move.

The twins' neighbor, Itrimobé, was in fact a fearsome, man-eating monster. He swiftly appeared and snatched an immobilized Ikotobekibo.

STOP! PLEASE! I'M SORRY!

Itrimobé brought the terrified Ikotobekibo into his house and tied him to a post. Itrimobé planned to save the boy to eat for later.

Ifaramalemy sought the counsel of a wise man for a way to free her brother from the monster. The wise man shared that the mighty Itrimobé's greatest weakness was his paralyzing fear of cats.

Armed with a plan, she hid in a hole in Itrimobé's wall. When Itrimobé entered his house, Ifaramalemy began meowing like a little cat.

Itrimobé was so horrified of cats that he immediately turned and bolted out of his house at a frenzied pace. In his panic, he paid little attention to his surroundings.

He was so frightened and ran so fast that he did not even realize he was headed toward a deep ravine.

He ran straight off the edge and fell to his death.

After Itrimobé died, the orphans, Ifaramalemy and Ikotobekibo, laid claim to his property.

Ikotobekibo, overcome with gratitude for his sister having saved his life, decided to make sure that her needs were met before his own. Their health improved and together they shared the abundance of their new garden with the people of their community.

MORE BANANAS, SISTER?

YES, PLEASE! THANK YOU.

Josia

Antananarivo

Madagasikara lies to the east of the African continent in the Indian Ocean and is the fourth largest island in the world. Current research suggests that there were three central migrations that occurred from Island Southeast Asia to Madagasikara beginning in the third century BC with the arrival of taro, yam, banana, and rice. The second but primary migration for settlement occurred around 500 to 700 AD, and a final migration era existed during the twelfth to fifteenth centuries AD. Modern Malagasy populations of Madagasikara possess an equal admixture of Island Southeast Asia Austronesian and East African ancestry. Also, the Malagasy language shares about 90 percent of its basic lexicon with the Ma'anyan language spoken in southern Borneo.

My hometown is Anjanahary in Antananarivo, the capital of Madagasikara. In school, I learned that the Malagasy people came from Indonesia, Africa, and Arabia. I also learned of Malagasy customs that I had yet to experience.

CLASS, WHAT COUNTRY IS BORNEO ISLAND IN?

INDONESIA?

BORNEO IS ACTUALLY SHARED BY INDONESIA, MALAYSIA, AND BRUNEI.

Incredibly, our Austronesian ancestors traveled on outrigger canoes all the way across the Indian Ocean to reach our shores!

Once on land, they encountered strange plants and animals that they had never seen before. Like the *baobab*, large-trunked native deciduous trees, and the *lemur*, an endemic primate.

It is said that when the first settlers arrived from the islands of Indonesia, there were already people living here in Madagasikara. They were called the Vazimba. As kids we were told that they still exist but have since become less like small-statured people and more like monsters!

We had to be careful when we went to the countryside or to areas like lakes, rivers, and scrublands because of them. My father told me that once as a schoolboy he saw a Vazimba behind some bushes. It had glowing red eyes!

AAACK! IT'S . . . A . . . VAZIMBA!

The common belief in Madagasikara is that the spirits of the dead still live among us and we need to honor them by obeying customary rules, *fady*. For instance, the ceremony of *famadihana* involves opening the tomb, taking out the body (or bones), and asking for a blessing, then rewrapping the bones with a new linen shroud and placing them back in the tomb. This is a big ceremony here.

On the island of Sulawesi, the Toraja people practice lavish funerals, which can include the killing of many water buffaloes and days of ritual. The *ma'nene* ceremony is when Torajan families exhume the bodies of their relatives and dress them in new clothes. It is a period of togetherness, where families take pictures and spend time with their deceased loved ones. This reminds me of the *famadihana* here in Madagasikara.

When I was eleven years old, I went to stay with my uncle and his family during summer break. They lived in Mangarivotra, Mahajanga, about a day's trip away from where we lived in Antananarivo. This was my first opportunity to visit and spend quality time with them.

My uncle and aunt lived in a newer house in Mahajanga. I was elated to see them when I finally arrived.

BONJOUR, JOSIA!

BONJOUR.

BONJOUR!

My aunt prepared all the meals for the day in the morning. She cooked rice and *sides*. The *sides* were side dishes consisting of meat, vegetables, green leaves, etc.

There were many people living in their house. My uncle would go to work in the morning and come home for lunch, then head back to work. We all ate about two-thirds of the *sides* for lunch, and a third was kept for dinner. At dinner, my uncle would eat first. When he was satisfied . . .

. . . whatever was left would be for the rest of us. If he was cheerful, he would eat less and give most of the meal to the family; but, if he was exhausted and starving, he might eat all the food and the rest of us would only get rice!

This is a traditional form of respect and honor given to the head of the family.

23

For me, the *Famadihana* is a way for Malagasy people to show respect for their ancestors and that even though they have died, they continue to be honored and loved. The way the Vazimba legends are used is for fear so that we obey our traditions. I have negative thoughts about some of the *Fady* laws . . . doing this, not doing that. . . . Usually, the consequence for not performing the tradition is shared . . .

. . . but the blessing for following the *Fady* is not really known.

I often reflected on the significance of my uncle and aunt's dinner tradition growing up. It was quite shocking at first, but I believe that it instills gratitude for one's parents, especially those who work tirelessly to provide for their families—hardworking parents like my uncle and aunt.

MANAO AHOANA!

Now, being a parent myself, I have come to see this tradition in a more positive light as a symbolic gesture of appreciation by the family. Madagasikara is an incredibly beautiful place, full of history and tradition. I am proud of my Malagasy heritage!

Part III: My Mountain

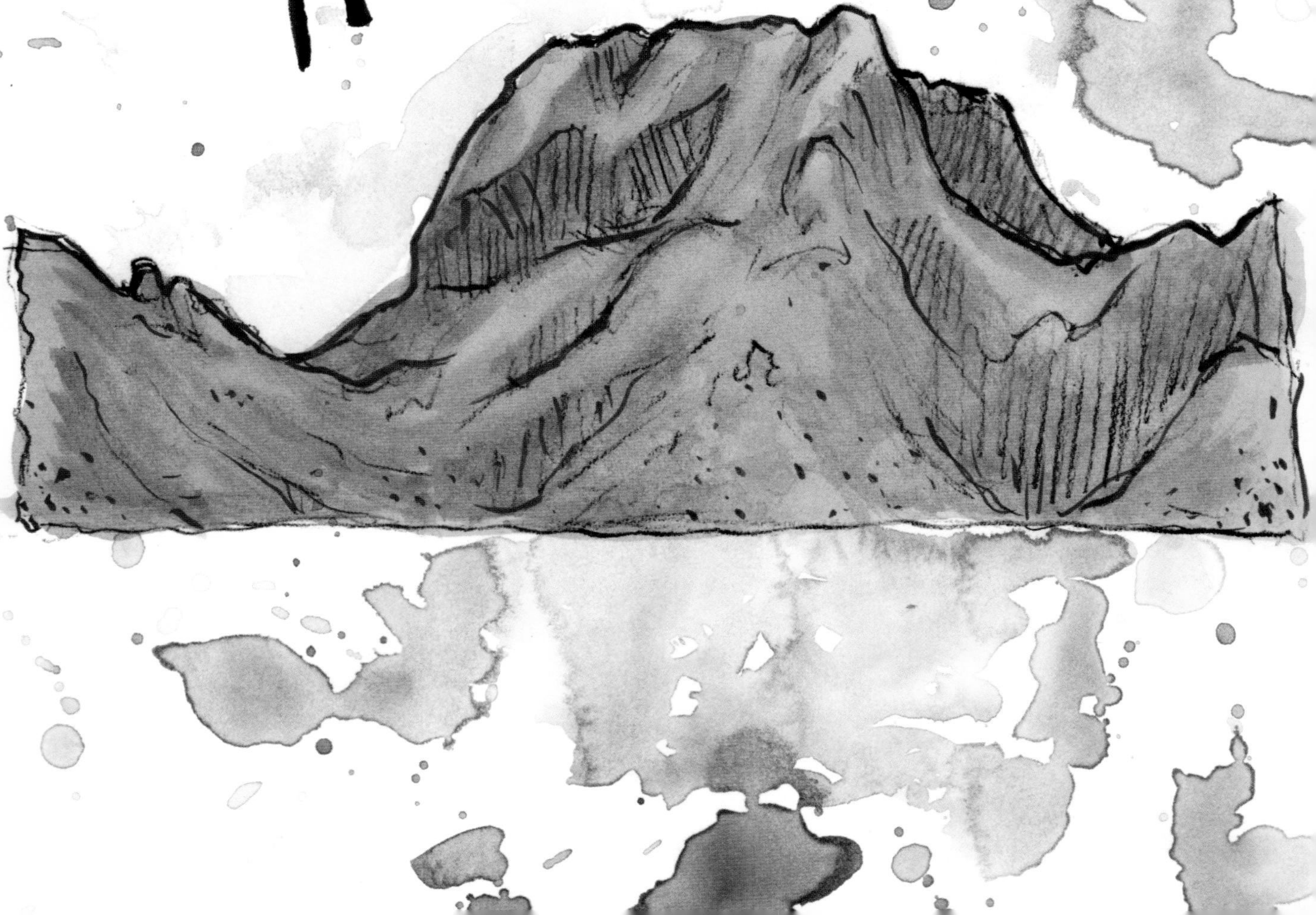

Chantelle

My family and I moved to Tutuila, American Samoa, from Utah when I was just a teenager. In reflecting on my experiences in Samoa, there are a few memories that stand out.

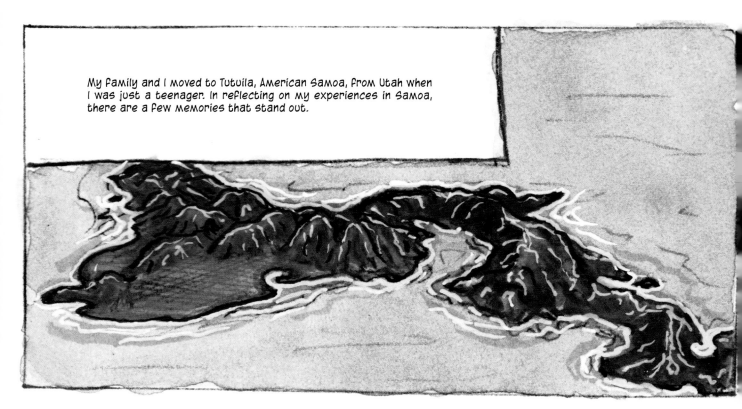

I remember seeing the many *faleo'o*, traditional Samoan houses with their open walls. How different this was from Utah.

When we first arrived, we lived at the famous Rainmaker Hotel nestled in 'Utulei with views of Mount Pioa, Rainmaker Mountain, across Pago Pago Harbor.

I recall trying to avoid all the *fefe* grass, *Mimosa pudica*, and the giant poisonous toads when I walked around at night.

I also remember my first frightening encounters with flying cockroaches! Good thing they had even bigger *mo'o*, lizards!

CRUNCH

My grandparents had moved back to Tutuila from Utah two years before we did. My grandpa was deeply rooted and strong in his Samoan culture.

When we moved to Samoa, things that I had learned growing up in Utah about Samoa suddenly had context, take medical care for instance.

Once, I had a severe case of boils on my toes that even surgery could not fix. My grandpa, however, knew traditional Samoan medicine.

He took special leaves, chewed them up, and then spit them on my ailing toes.

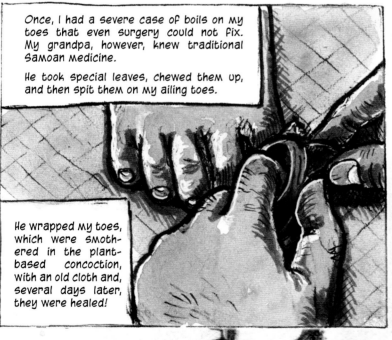

He wrapped my toes, which were smothered in the plant-based concoction, with an old cloth and, several days later, they were healed!

American Samoa's biggest industry is tuna canning. I still clearly remember the pungent aroma of processed tuna wafting through the moist tropical air.

One afternoon, I was at Two Dollar beach with my cheerleader friends from high school. My grandpa, who was a painter, was there too and wanted to wash the paint off himself after work.

He swam out from the beach all the way to the deepest part of the ocean. He was like a fish. He was so happy to be back home. Grandpa loved the ocean.

At certain points during my time in American Samoa, I would go up to the mountains high above Pago Pago Harbor to stay with my grandparents. There were no paved roads or sidewalks leading there. Instead, I had to hike up an incredibly steep mountain trail that eventually led across a bubbling stream, all the while keeping an eye out for roving island dogs, to reach where they lived.

The good thing about such a long journey was that my grandparents always had hot food waiting for me.

My grandparents' house was constructed from an old Matson shipping container with a tin roof put over the top of it. Their floor was made of concrete and crushed coral, and the house was surrounded by lush tropical vegetation.

EEEK! SO COLD!

My grandparents did not own a TV, instead they had a makeshift boombox. An old kerosene lamp illuminated the house at night and there were doilies everywhere. At breakfast, Grandpa liked to mix Postum, a coffee sub-stitute, in a bowl with cabin crackers and butter!

If I wanted to take a shower, I had to go outside and stand under a pipe that was connected to a cistern, which collected FREEZING COLD MOUNTAIN WATER! Showers were both a dreadful and exhilarating experience!

The panoramic views of Pago Pago Harbor from my grandparents' mountain house were breathtaking. Tutuila Island is blessed with tremendous natural beauty.

When I would finally head back down from the mountain to my parents' house, I would have to catch a ride on the very colorful and equally noisy 'aiga buses. The 'aiga bus is a form of transportation unique to American Samoa.

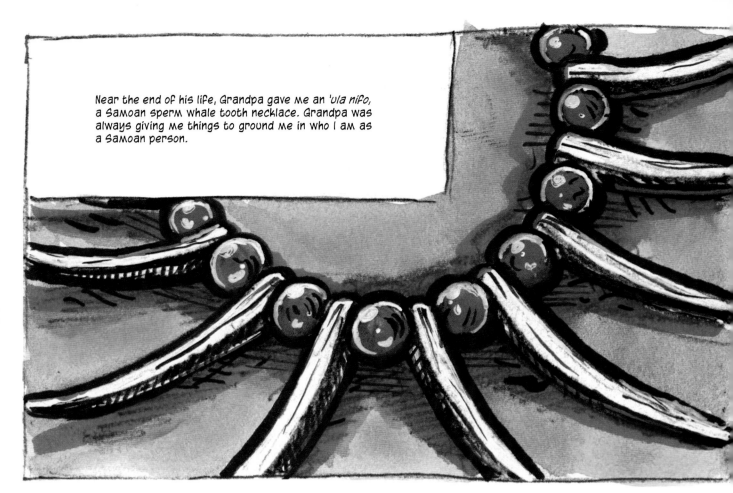

Near the end of his life, Grandpa gave me an *'ula nifo*, a Samoan sperm whale tooth necklace. Grandpa was always giving me things to ground me in who I am as a Samoan person.

Even though I do not speak fluent *Gagana Sāmoa*, Samoan language, my upbringing was unequivocally culturally Samoan. We had Samoan weddings, *fa'alavelave, lauga,* and *malaga.* I had and continue to have many traditional Samoan responsibilities. This is not a uniform that I can simply remove at the end of the day, being Samoan is who I am.

Part IV:

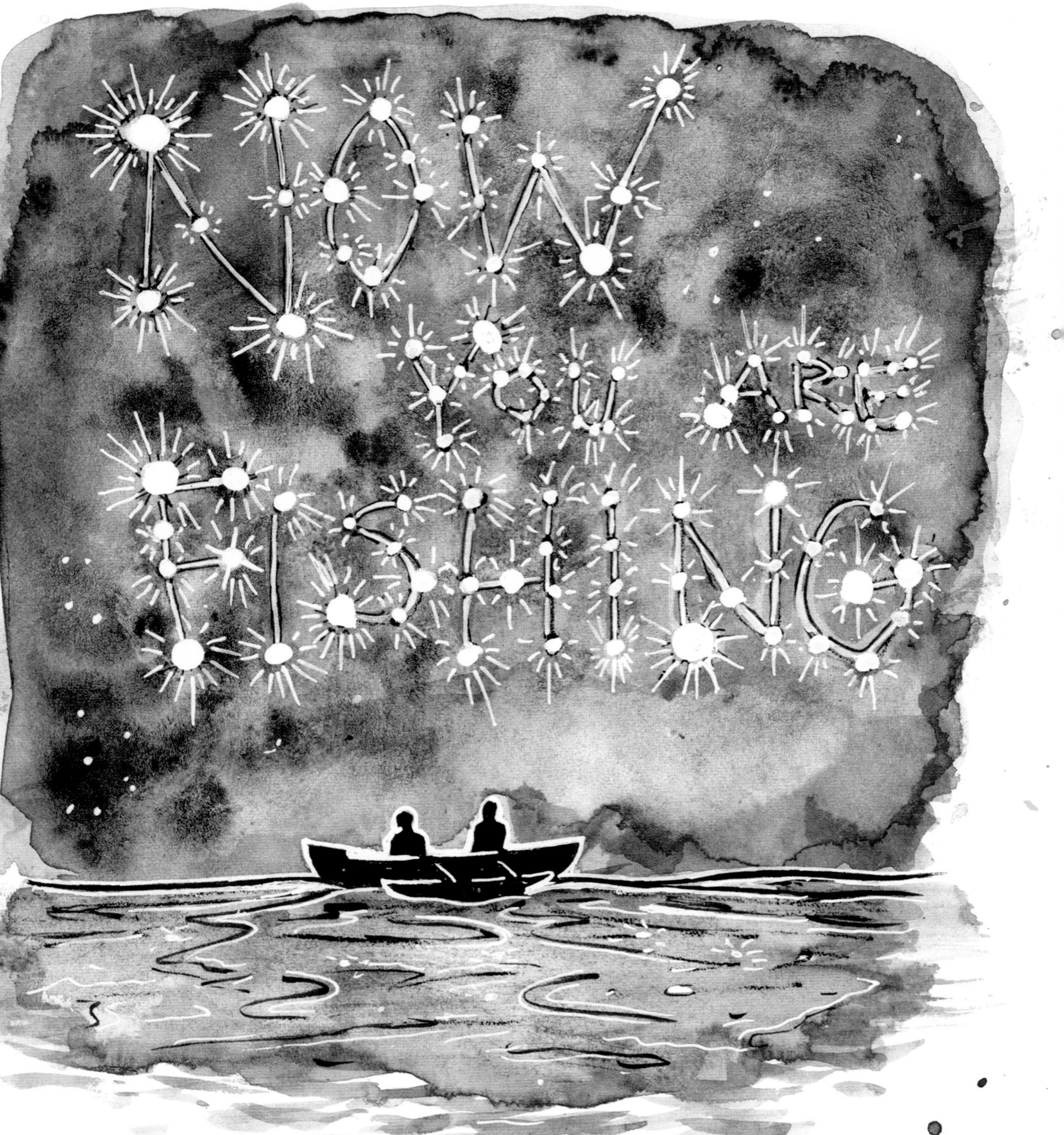
NOW YOU ARE FISHING

Viata

My story starts long ago on the island of Banaba, also called Ocean Island, which was once rich in phosphate.

Tapiwa

Banaba

Many people from Kiribati and Tuvalu worked on Banaba mining the phosphate in the early twentieth century. The Banabans were exploited, and their phosphate used to enrich countries like Britain, Australia, and New Zealand.

On Banaba, my Kiribati grandfather worked as a mechanic supervisor. My Tuvaluan grandmother was a nurse. Her father, the head of police, disliked my Kiribati grandfather because he was not Tuvaluan, but that did not stop my grandparents from dating and eventually getting married. Afterward, they moved to Tarawa.

Tabwakea
London
Paris
Poland
Banana
Kiritimati

A generation later, my family ended up on Kiritimati Island in Kiribati. I was born and raised on Kiritimati Island. I am descended from navigators and Kiritimati Island is my home.

I remember when I was young, my father would take me out on fishing trips to the sea on *te wa*, the canoe.

My father, Takaeang, was an excellent fisherman and his father was a very skilled navigator. They were from the outer island of Onotoa. They could read the signs of the clouds and the sea. I was told by my grandfather that if I wanted to become a navigator, I needed to spend time fishing with my father. My father possessed an intimate understanding of the ocean, the stars, and swells.

DAD, MAYBE WE SHOULD STOP HERE? . . . I CAN BARELY SEE THE LAND NOW! IT'S SO DARK AND THE SWELLS ARE HUGE!

VIATA, WE HAVE NOT STARTED FISHING YET. IT IS ONLY FISHING WHEN YOU LOSE SIGHT OF LAND AND ARE SURROUNDED ONLY BY THE SEA.

My father called fishing, "the disappearance of land."

Part V: Pito

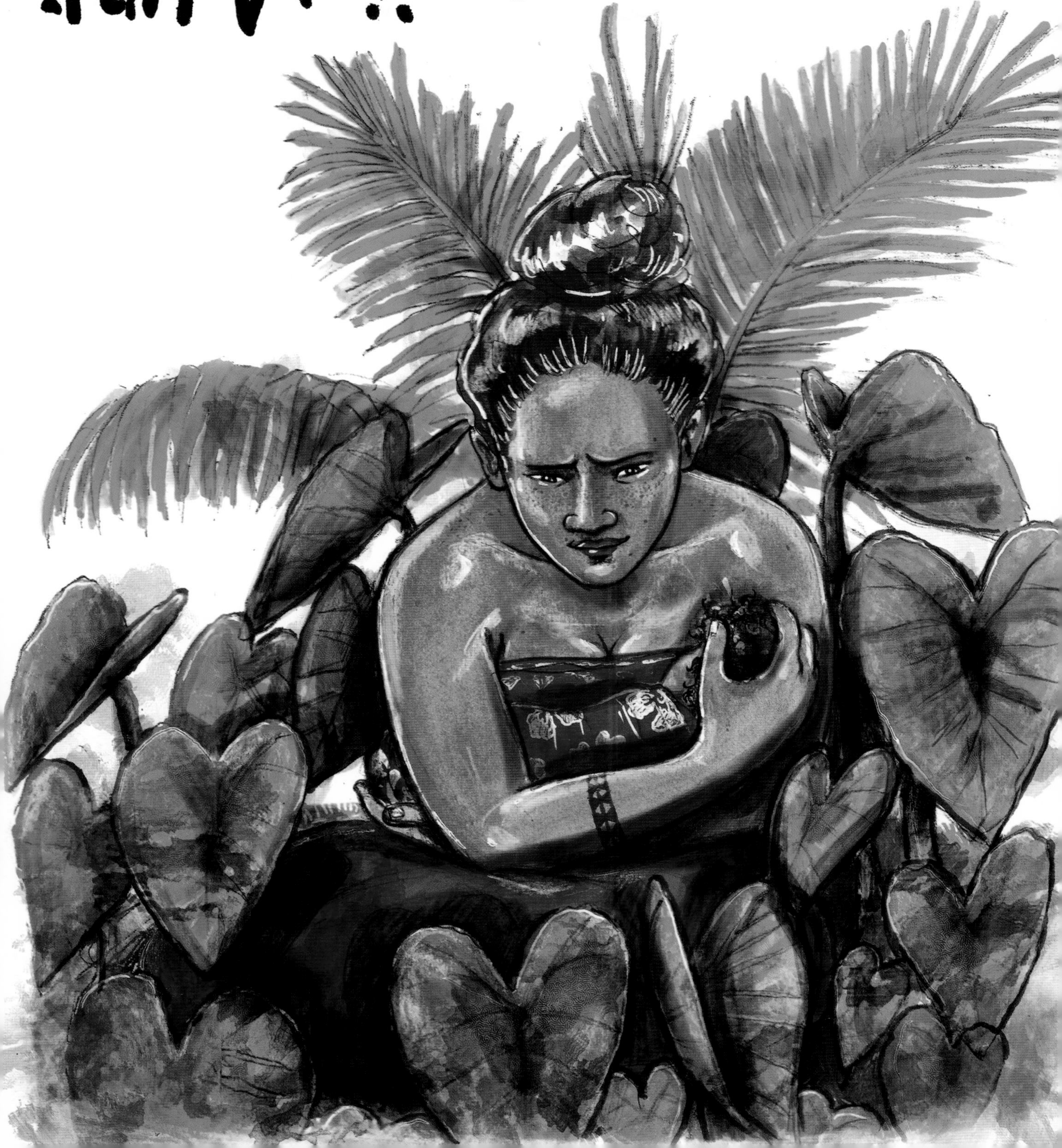

We cannot read our histories without knowing how to read our landscapes (and seascapes)... They often inspire in us a sense of reverence and awe, not to mention fear and revulsion. These are reasons why it is essential not to destroy our landmarks, for with their removal very important parts of our memories, our histories, will be erased.

It may be significant in this regard
that in several Austronesian
languages the word for "placenta" and "womb"
is also the word for "land." The womb
nurtures and protects the unborn child, as the
land nurtures and provides security for
humanity. At the end, the departed are
returned to the womb of the land...
People are one with their culture and land.

— Epeli Hau'ofa, 2008

Bali: In the village of Bayung Gede, the people believe that their ancestors first emerged from *tued kayu*, the trunk of a tree, brought forth by Bhatara Bayu, the wind god. As an homage to their origin, the people of Bayung Gede attach the *ari-ari*, placenta, of a newborn child to the *bukak* tree located in the *setra ari-ari*, or placenta cemetery. A large *nyuh*, coconut, shell is divided in two and the *ari-ari* is placed inside along with some spices and ceremonial items, then sealed with lime. *Salang tabu*, bamboo rope, is used to bind the coconut shell halves together. The child's father brings the *nyuh* to *setra ari-ari* and hangs it from the *bukak* tree as they have done for millennia.

The *ari-ari* is considered one of the *kanda pat*, four siblings, of the newborn. In other parts of Bali, the *ari-ari* is washed clean, wrapped gently in a white fabric, and placed inside a large *nyuh*, coconut, called a *wadah ari-ari*. This is then ceremonially buried, *nanem ari-ari*, somewhere around the family compound according to tradition. Some bury the *nyuh* at the entryway of their family compound and place a large rock on top of it, whilst others may bury it outside the kitchen. The family will continue to give offerings at this location to benefit the child.

Vuhul: In Vuhul and its surrounding islands, the traditions of caring for the *pūsud*, umbilical cord, and *inunlan*, placenta, of the *vāta*, baby, are varied in accordance with *varanggai*, village, or *vānai*, family. Generally, after a *vāta* is *gipangānak*, born, their *inahan/nānai*, mother, or *amahan/tātai*, father, take the *pūsud* and bury the *inunlan* in a damp, well-watered place. Some bury it next to a *luvi*, coconut tree, or other plants. The *pūsud*, on the other hand, is wrapped in a triangular cloth known as a *vigkis* and tied to the *salagunting*, rafters, of the *vālai*, house. The reason that the *inunlan* is buried in the *iūta*, land, of the family is to manifest a sacred connection between the *anāk*, child, and their ancestral domain.

Viti: In Viti, great importance, ceremony, and symbolism is bestowed upon the part of the umbilical cord closest to the navel, known as the *wa ni vicovico*. After giving birth, the child's *tina-na/nana*, mother, will remain at home and recover with her *gone*, child. The *tokatoka*, placenta, is given to the *momo*, maternal uncle, to dispose of. The *tama-na/tata*, father, will take the important *wa ni vicovico*, and will bury it in their *vanua*, family land, often next to a *niu*, coconut tree, or another tree, such as a *kulu*, breadfruit, sapling. This act intimately connects the child to the tree, their people, and their *vanua*.

Aotearoa: The *Te Reo Māori* words for land and placenta are the same, *whenua*. After the *pēpi*, baby, is born, the *whānau*, family, take the *whenua* of the *pēpi* and bury it in ancestral land. It is sometimes placed in an *ipu whenua*, afterbirth container, made of a *hue*, gourd. This, as in other Austronesian cultures, signifies one's lifelong connection to their land, *whenua*. The umbilical cord consists of three sections. That closest to the navel is known as the *pito*, the central portion is known as the *iho*, and the part closest to the placenta is known as the *rauru*. The *pito* can be tied, placed in a cloth, and then buried or put in the hollow of a sacred, *tapu*, tree, stone crevice, or boundary post. The *iho* is also tied with cordage and either buried in ancestral land or within the hollow, or at the base, of a *tapu* tree. The practices and traditions vary between *hapū*, clan/subtribe, and each is imbued with a unique sense of profound sacredness.

Part VI:

Paramountcy

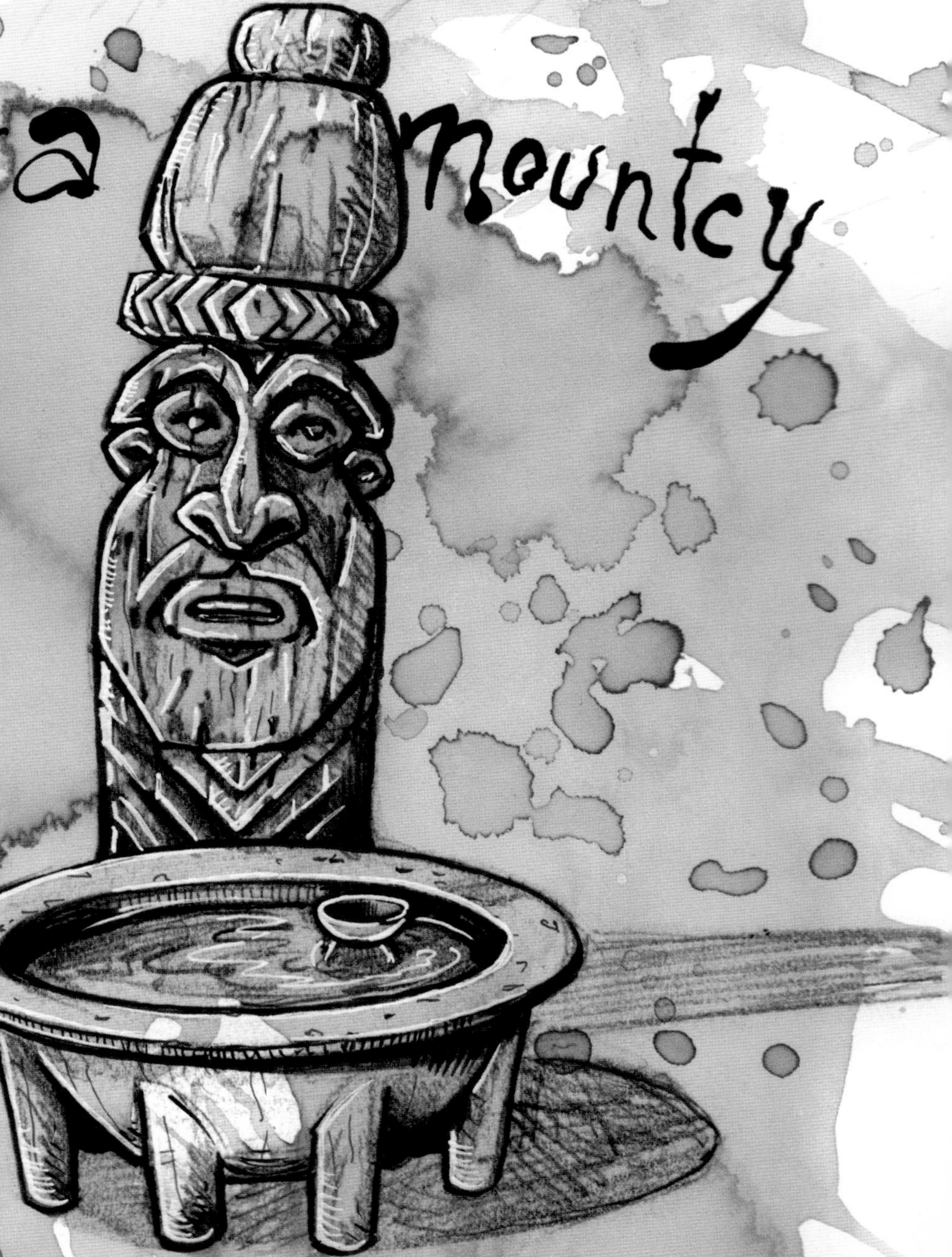

David

Some time ago, I went with a good friend of mine to a small village in Kanaky for a fishing trip. There, I learned about traditional Kanak marine tenure.

OUR FAMILIES HAVE RIGHTS OVER THE LAND, THE SHORE, AND EVEN THE SEA.

THE SEA?

YES, EACH FAMILY HAS STORY LINES IN THE SEA.

He meant that each rock and coral had stories connected to a family's genealogy and determined boundaries.

THE KANAK PEOPLE ARE THE FIRST PEOPLE OF THIS LAND AND WE NEED TO FOLLOW THEIR PROTOCOLS AND CUSTOMS.

As we sat at the café, my friend Sako explained his vision of everyone sitting around the kava bowl together, recognizing the paramountcy of the Kanak. Sako said that as Pacific Peoples we need to first follow traditional Kanak protocols and if we have good relations, then it is up to the Kanak to choose what they will share with us. That is the Pacific way.

Part VII:
Coconut Origins

Hina and the Eel

There was once a beautiful
woman named Hina who lived
in Tahiti. She was betrothed
to the King of Lake Vaihiria.
When she saw the king,
however, she was repulsed
by his appearance for he was
an enormous eel! She fled and
beseeched Māui, the demigod, for
help. Māui used his fishhook to
catch the giant eel. The Eel King
prophesied that Hina would one
day kiss him in desperation.
Māui then hacked the eel to pieces
and placed the head in a basket that he
gave to Hina. Māui warned Hina to keep the
head covered and to not let it touch the ground
until she had reached her village or else the
prophecy may come true. On her way home, Hina
became overheated. She set the basket down
on the ground while she cooled down in a nearby
river. The ground swallowed the basket and soon
after a strange tree began to grow in that
spot. It was the first coconut tree. Sometime
later, a devastating drought enveloped Tahiti.
Dying of thirst, Hina took a coconut from the
tree and shook it. She could tell there was
liquid inside. She husked the coconut,
which revealed two eyes and a mouth.
Hina pressed her lips to it to drink.
She then recalled the prophecy, for
the coconut was the head of the
Eel King and she had indeed kissed
him in desperation.

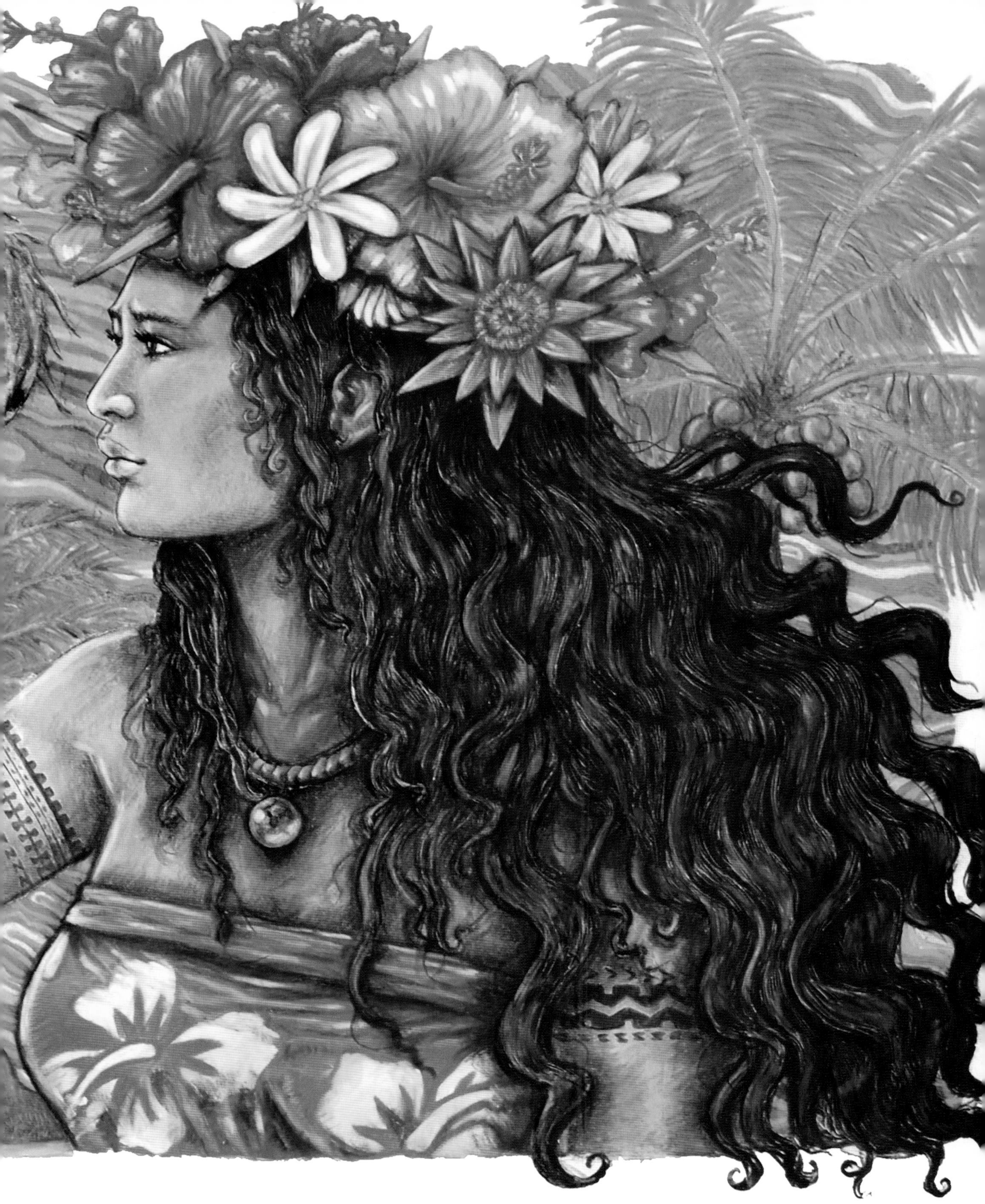

I Trongkon Niyok

Long, long ago on Guåhan, there lived a CHamoru family from the Achote tribe who had a daughter, *iha*, renowned for her incredible beauty. She had a deep love for her people and desired to help provide for their needs. Everyone in the village greatly admired her. One day, the young woman was suddenly struck with an insatiable thirst that no drink could quench.

Despite the village's best efforts, she continued to grow increasingly ill.

She told them of a special fruit growing from a strange tree.

She said that the juice from this enigmatic fruit would satiate her thirst and cure her. She described the tree and its fruit in detail, but no one had ever heard of or seen such a plant. Regardless, the young woman's father, *tåta*, and mother, *nåna*, along with all the villagers desperately searched the island, but to no avail.

The young woman died soon after. Her *tåta* buried her on a high hill overlooking their village. Everyone was burdened with agonizing grief.

Some time later, her *tåta*, *nåna*, and several villagers went to visit the young woman's grave. They were shocked to find a peculiar plant growing from the head of the grave.

HÅFA AYU?!

Believing it to be of magical derivation, the villagers constructed a shelter to protect the mysterious plant. They continued to watch it as it grew ever taller each passing year.

After five years, clusters of round fruit appeared beneath the branches. One fell to the ground. The *tåta* shook the fruit and heard sloshing inside. The chief asked the *tåta* to taste the fruit, but after peeling away the outer husk he noticed a face beneath and declined.

The dead woman's *nåna* believed that the fruit was a divine gift and drank the juice. It was refreshing and sweet to the taste. She opened the fruit and ate the white meat inside, which was delicious as well. The *tåta* and the other villagers were thrilled.

This was the origin of the first coconut tree on Guåhan and since those ancient times the CHamoru People have relied on it for hydration, sustenance, ropes, building and weaving materials, among other uses. The young woman who had greatly loved her people continues to provide for their needs to this day.

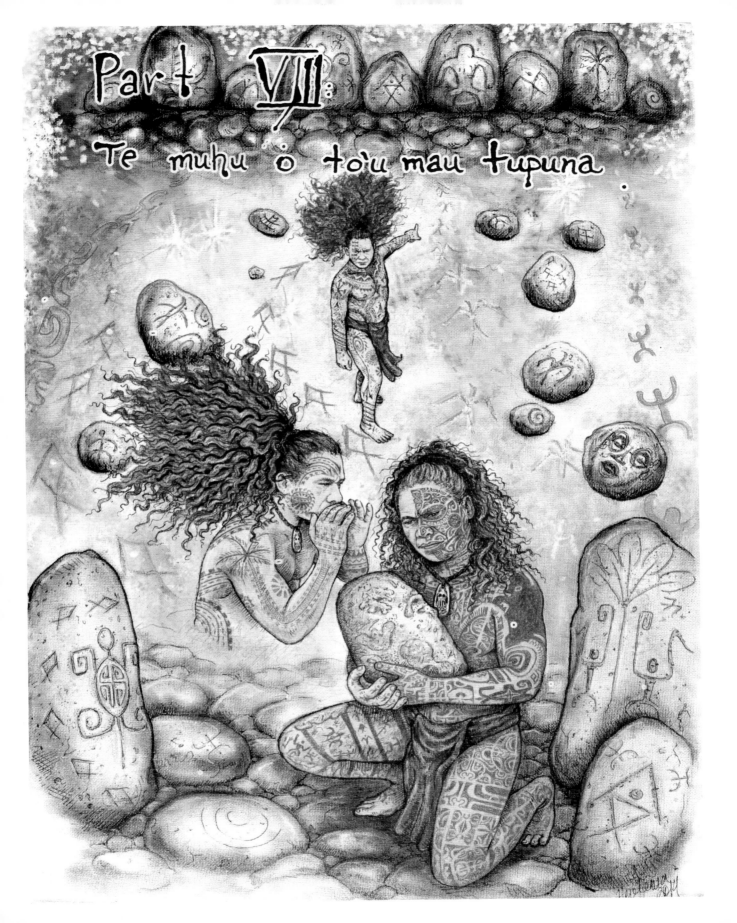

Part VII:

Te muhu ò toʻu mau tupuna.

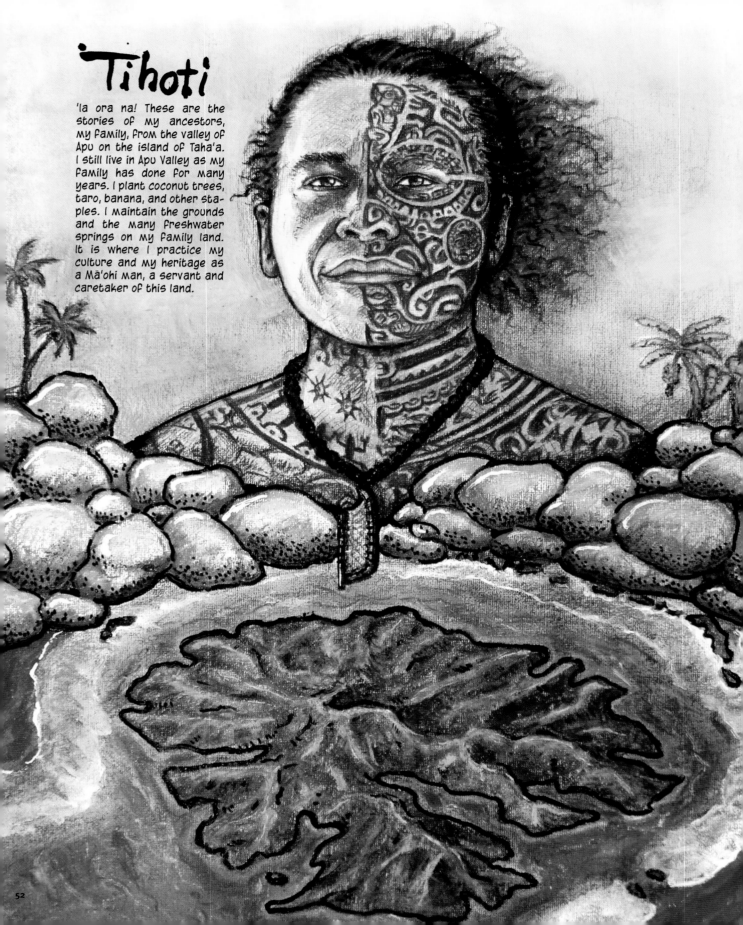

Tihoti

'Ia ora na! These are the stories of my ancestors, my family, from the valley of Apu on the island of Taha'a. I still live in Apu Valley as my family has done for many years. I plant coconut trees, taro, banana, and other staples. I maintain the grounds and the many freshwater springs on my family land. It is where I practice my culture and my heritage as a Mā'ohi man, a servant and caretaker of this land.

Apu Valley is located next to Apu Bay on the southern side of Taha'a Island. In the 1920s and '30s, many people worked as fishermen and farmers. They also harvested coconuts for copra.

The valley had many freshwater springs. They were about one meter deep with many bubbles.

The cold water still flows in these cleansing springs today.

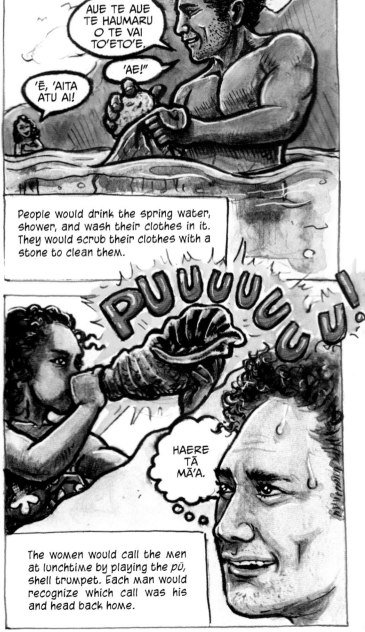

AUE TE AUE TE HAUMARU O TE VAI TO'ETO'E.

'AE!"

'Ē, 'AITA ATU AI!

People would drink the spring water, shower, and wash their clothes in it. They would scrub their clothes with a stone to clean them.

PUUUUUUU!

HAERE TĀ MĀ'A.

The women would call the men at lunchtime by playing the pū, shell trumpet. Each man would recognize which call was his and head back home.

In those days, the village of Apu had no electricity and the morning alarm clock was the rooster. All the men would head off early to the valley to work.

E, 'IA ORA NA!

E, E 'IA ORA NA.

My grandmother, Tera'ivahine, was a *tahu'a*, a healer. She used plant medicine to heal the sick. This was Mā'ohi health care.

"A PARAI I TE MŌNO'I TĀMANU."

No money needed. The forest was our pharmacy.

They shared their food and never worried about money. When they planted and cleaned the banana trees they always prayed. They were very respectful of nature.

When my grandfather was sixteen in the 1930s, he went fishing with his friend and his friend's father in an old *va'a*, Tahitian canoe, with paddles and sails. They left from Taha'a to Bora Bora.

E MANUIA TE TAUTAI I TEIE MAHANA.

TE PIRI MAI RA TĀTOU IA VAVAU.

E T'IHI TĀ'OE E Ā'AHI TĀ'U !

My grandfather and his friend were excited to catch fish. The father of my grandfather's friend guided the canoe with the two boys to somewhere near the halfway point in the channel between the two islands of Taha'a and Bora Bora.

54

TE FA'ARUMARUMA TE RA'I !

The father saw big clouds coming from Bora Bora. He told the boys they needed to head back.

But the boys wanted to stay where they were and continue fishing.

E PĀ INO, MEA AMU TE I'A.

'AORE E MAU.

CRAACK...!!

Soon after, a great storm was upon them. The wind blew strong, causing violent, crashing waves. The storm waves hit the canoe hard and destroyed the *ama*, outrigger.

They were drifting to Bora Bora around 5 p.m. This was a big problem. So, the father went to the back of the canoe and prayed in an ancient Tahitian tongue. The boys thought it sounded like he was calling for something.

A few minutes later, they felt the canoe push up slightly out of the water. They began to slowly move toward the island of Taha'a.

At around 8 p.m., they arrived back in Apu on Taha'a. The people of the village lit fires on the beach to guide them home.

E, TO MĀTOU TĀURA MAEVA NUI IA 'OE.

When my grandfather and his friend looked back at the lagoon, they saw a huge *ma'o*, shark! The father had called for his *tāura*, ancestral guardian spirit, to help them, and his *tāura* came and guided their canoe.

Tāura can come in the form of a *ma'o* . . .

. . . *honu*, sea turtle . . .

. . . *manu*, bird . . .

. . . or, even a *fai*, stingray.

Many years later, during his funeral, a big *ma'o* and *fai* came in close to the beach, then turned away. They were saying goodbye.

When my dad and uncle were teenagers, they had to go catch fish in the lagoon for the family's dinner. They were the oldest of the children, so they were required to help their parents.

Before they went fishing, my dad would gather the dried *nī'au*, coconut leaves. He would collect around fifteen branches, then tie them together, and carry them on his back.

My uncle carried a bucket and knife on his back. My dad would burn one *ni'au* at a time. The fire attracted the fish in the lagoon and my uncle would whack them!

NAVA'I?

E, NAVA'I ROA.

On moonless nights, they could fill up their bucket with fish in about an hour. They would then head happily back home to cook and eat with the family.

They would watch the *rava'ai*, fishermen, paddle their canoes out in the lagoon at night. The *rava'ai* would use the *mōrī teitei*, a kerosene lamp with a pump. There was a certain place in the lagoon where the fish would congregate before reaching the outer reef. They would bait them with *tupa*, crab. The lights on the canoes could be seen from land. They would stick the fish, such as jackfish, with three-pronged *pātia*, spears. My grandfather as an old man was an expert spear thrower. I love stories about life in Taha'a back then.

Part IX
Recovering Culture

Hotu Matu'a

Long ago, Hau Maka had a dream where his spirit visited the then unknown island of Rapa Nui.

Hau Maka and his brother, Hua Tava, told King Matu'a of Hiva about the strange dream.

MY KING, TE PITO O TE KAIŊA A HAU MAKA IS THE EIGHTH AND LAST ISLAND OF THE TWILIGHT BEFORE THE RISING SUN. IT IS A NEW LAND FOR US.

In response, King Matu'a sent seven young men to find this new island in the southeast.

The men sailed far away and found it. On the slopes of Rano Kau, a man named Ku'uku'u planted yams.

AUE!!!

The men competed to lift a large honu, sea turtle. Ku'uku'u tried but it broke his back!

AUÉ!!

The other men abandoned the injured Ku'uku'u in a cave, where he ultimately died.

Afterward, the remaining men found a great surf spot on the west side of the island. Then, they returned to Hiva.

Back on Hiva, a rising tide was ruining the land.

MY SON, YOU MUST LEAVE NOW.

King Matu'a instructed his son, Hotu Matu'a, to migrate to the new island, Rapa Nui.

OHONA!

Hotu Matu'a gathered people, plants, and animals and set out on a six-week voyage.

As the group approached the new island, the canoe was split in two. One was led by Hotu Matu'a and the other by Hineriru.

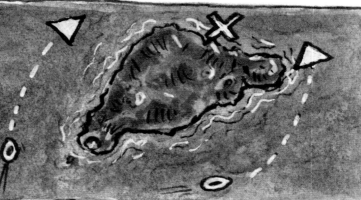

Hineriru went around the north and Hotu Matu'a went around the south. Both were trying to reach the landing at Anakena first.

As they neared Anakena, Hotu Matu'a cast a powerful spell that made his boat go faster and Hineriru's slower.

Hotu Matu'a and his wife, Vakai-a-hiva, landed at Anakena first. There, they had a son named, Tu'u Maheke. Hineriru brought the Rongorongo script. This is the origin of the Rapa Nui People.

Francisco

Every February, Rapa Nui holds a two-week cultural festival called Tapati. I have participated in a couple Tapati. Sometimes, I get more involved, like painting myself and accompanying the floats during the Farándula event. Farándula is a parade and in the 1960s was just like any other parade, people dressing in different costumes for fun, but now you must dress tradition-ally, well, traditional in a broad sense, since people experiment a lot with their costumes and body paint. The idea is not to wear shirts, *pareu*, waist wrap, or anything that does not look like it can be acquired directly from nature.

People wear bark cloth, feather headdresses, and other accessories. It's called *he 'a'ati rei rei kahu*, traditional costume making.

Then, people decorate themselves with traditional motifs using *kie'a*, a natural reddish pigment, along with other natural pigments. This *takona*, body painting, or *he tatu o te 'uka* is a way of expressing cultural designs.

There are many cultural events during the two weeks of Tapati, like the *tau'a*, marathon, and the *haka pei*. In the *haka pei*, competitors lay atop slippery banana trunks, then race down a grassy hill at 60 mph!

Á!!!

CHEEEEEHOOOOOOOO!

Today, many Chilean tourists are involved in Tapati, which I feel they use as an excuse to get dressed up and pretend to be Rapa Nui. On one hand, Tapati is a vehicle for cultural revival and expression; but . . .

On the other hand, tourism can also be used to exploit culture, particularly when tourists are permitted to perform Indigenous culture. It is a fine line to walk between.

Tapati is a fun festival and I do have a good time. I just sometimes wonder how it impacts Rapa Nui culture, particularly in recovering the culture from colonization. I wonder what the long-term impacts of mass tourism are in this relatively remote place.

Honestly, I adore Rapa Nui. I love the island, the Rapa Nui People, and culture. Though the island is not large, it is well connected to the outside world.

The beauty of Rapa Nui's rolling grassy terrain, and the high cliffs that plunge into cobalt blue seas is calming to me. Rapa Nui is MY MAGNIFICENT ISLAND HOME.

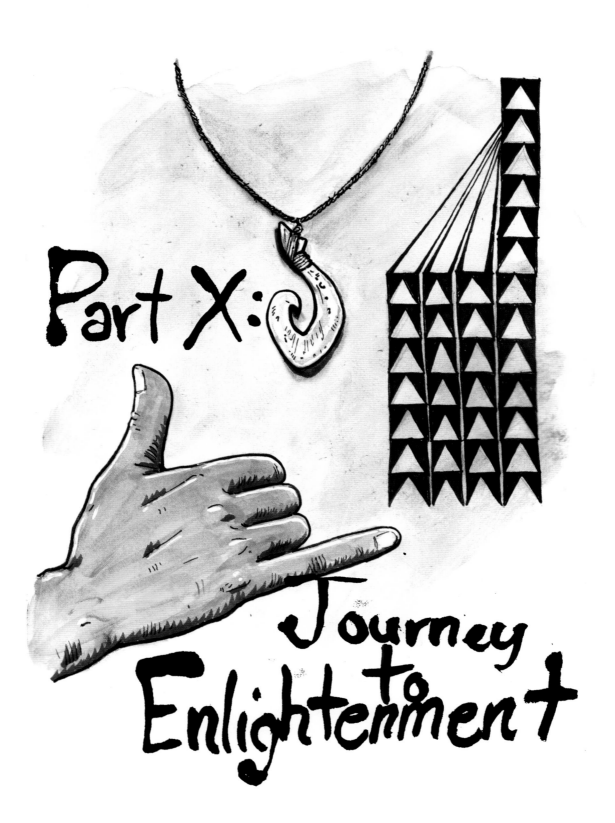

Part X: Journey to Enlightenment

Mike

A warm breeze blows across the lagoon through the *hala* trees into Mike's open-air island *dōjō*. Mike Stone is well known in the world of martial arts and now organizes martial arts philosophy courses for eager students from all around the world.

ALOHA E MIKE, WOULD YOU MIND TALKING STORY ABOUT GROWING UP IN HAWAI'I AND HOW YOU CAME TO LIVE HERE ON PANGLAU ISLAND?

ALOHA! I'D LOVE TO! WE SHOULD START AT THE BEGINNING.

I was born at 'Ewa Hospital in 1943 and grew up in Nānākuli on O'ahu's west side.

My parents met while my father was working as a merchant marine. He was originally from Tennessee. My father was White, and my mother was Native Hawaiian and Filipino.

My wonderful grandmother was fully Native Hawaiian. As a child growing up in Nānākuli, I began to identify strongly with my Polynesian ancestry, more so than my American nationality.

My grandfather, Amina, was a pastor, and most of my family was Pentecostal. My grandfather spoke often about love, but he was quite a harsh disciplinarian.

I remember that everyone at my grandfather's church was always crying.

We moved from Nānākuli to Maui when my father became a switchboard operator for the Maui Electric Company in 1949.

My father bought property across the street from Makawao Elementary School. We used to play in the schoolyard all the time. That is where I discovered my athleticism. About four miles from the school, in upcountry Makawao, was a place called Pi'iholo. Since we lived quite far from the sea, this was where we would go to swim.

One Friday after school when I was thirteen years old, my brother and I decided to go with three friends for a weekend camping trip to Pi'iholo. We packed canned food, blankets, matches, and headed out through the graveyard at St. Joseph's Catholic Church.

On our way, we picked huge pineapples from the plantation. We smashed them against rocks, peeled them open, and ate them fresh all the way up to Pi'iholo. We also gathered macadamia nuts, *waiawī,* and *liliko'i.*

At Pi'iholo there were three ponds called First Pond, Second Pond, and Honeymoon Pond. We reached Second Pond at around 3 p.m. There was this little cave next to it.

WE MADE IT!

While we were swimming, it started to become cloudy and then it started to drizzle.

Suddenly, it was a deluge! Everything got wet! We had not brought a tarpaulin, assuming it was going to be a sunny weekend.

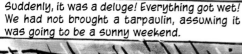

We hid out from the rain inside the cave. It was small but big enough for all of us to fit comfortably.

As night fell, we were freezing our *'ōkoles* off! We lit a fire, but only had a few pieces of dry firewood. As the rain continued to pour, the pond began to flood. The rising water threatened the entrance of our little cave.

We chose to eat everything we had packed in case the cave flooded. That was our first decision.

It was my *kuleana*, responsibility, as the eldest of the group to determine if we should stay. My father would be upset if we lost our things to the flood and I didn't want to drown either! While deciding, I recalled the ghost stories I had heard of the "White Lady" at Pi'iho-lo. For some reason, I imagined her wanting to help us survive that stormy night. The thought comforted me, so we stayed put and, fortunately, the rising waters never flooded the cave.

Early the next morning while it was still dark, the rain stopped, and the sky cleared. The sun came up, we dried out, foraged, and had a fantastic weekend. The "White Lady" was watching out for us after all.

Looking back, I am glad that we stuck it out and stayed even though things were not going well. That was a defining moment in my life.

Fast-forward to when I joined the army a couple of weeks after graduating high school. I was nineteen years old and freshly stationed at Fort Chaffee, Arkansas, where I met my karate instructor.

I loved karate and won every match that I entered. After only six months of training, I won at nationals.

The judges could not believe that a brown belt had won. They accused my instructor of demoting me from a black belt to a brown belt when in fact I was only a white belt at the time!

Following my unexpected victory, my instructor presented me with a black belt.

When my time in the military was over, I moved to California and taught at Ed Parker's karate school. I then started my own school in Los Alamitos.

I went on to promote over fifty martial arts shows between Hawai'i and the US Mainland.

WHAT AM I GONNA DO WITH MY LIFE? I'VE ACHIEVED EVERYTHING THAT I'VE WANTED TO IN MARTIAL ARTS. MOST PEOPLE THINK MARTIAL ARTS SHOULD TAKE A LIFETIME OF HARD WORK, SUFFERING, AND SACRIFICE; I SUCCEEDED WITHOUT ANY OF THAT! IT'S BECAUSE I KNOW WHO I AM, MY TRUE NATURE. MAYBE, I CAN SHARE MY NEW PHILOSOPHY AND MENTALITY WITH OTHERS TO HELP THEM FIND THEMSELVES. BUT WHERE CAN I FIND A PEACEFUL PLACE TO TEACH THEM?

After I wrote the script for *Enter the Ninja*, I came to the Philippines in 1981 to shoot the film. I ended up staying behind to do other projects, still looking for that "place."

By 1986, I was set to film another movie but then the overthrow of the Marcos regime occurred. The production company called me at my hotel in Manila.

THE PEOPLE ARE GATHERING IN THE THOUSANDS ON EDSA.

DON'T COME BACK TO AMERICA JUST YET.

Taina, my girlfriend, asked me to visit her home island since I suddenly had free time.

MIKE, MY ISLAND HAS BEAUTIFUL BEACHES!

TAINA, I'M FROM HAWAI'I. PLEASE DON'T TELL ME ABOUT BEAUTIFUL BEACHES!

We took a prop plane and landed in Tagvilaran.

We drove across Panglao Island on our way to Dulho, on the island's southwestern tip.

The moment I walked out on the beach at Dulhu, I was in awe. It was a kilometer long with not a soul in sight. Powdery white sand, clear turquoise water. The owner was a friend of my girlfriend's father. He went by the nickname, "Colonel."

HONESTLY, I WOULD LOVE TO BUY SOME OF THIS BEACHFRONT FROM YOU, COLONEL.

WELL, YOU SEEM NICE, BUT I'M NOT SO SURE. I WANTED TO LEAVE MOST OF IT TO MY CHILDREN.

SO, IF I SELL YOU A PIECE OF MY LAND, WILL YOU MOVE HERE TO LIVE?

YES, OF COURSE. THIS PLACE IS PARADISE!

I respected that the Colonel did not want to sell, and I thought nothing more of it. That next Sunday, however, we came back to attend a party he was throwing. The Colonel was in particularly good spirits and had given my offer more thought. He told me to get into a *vanka* and point out the land that I wanted.

RIGHT THERE, THAT PIECE OF LAND BETWEEN THE TWO COCONUT TREES IS PERFECT!

I wanted to live in Dulhu because it was just like Nānākuli in the old days, where I grew up. I saw it as a place where I could remove myself from modern distraction and focus on living and teaching my martial arts and life philosophy. When I walked out on the beach, it reminded me of Grandfather Amina's place. He used to take care of the Nānāikapono Elementary School grounds near where he lived by the beach.

I WILL SELL YOU MY LAND ON THE CONDITION THAT YOU MOVE HERE AND MARRY TAINA.

THERE'S NO WAY! WE'VE ONLY JUST STARTED DATING!

Three years later, Taina and I were married. We went back to see the Colonel. He smiled and sold us the land.

Everything about Panglau Island felt familiar some-how—the way the kids played using sticks, slippers, bicycle tires, whatever they could find, running around everywhere without fear, families taking care of one another, sharing what they had. It was as if I were reliving my childhood at age forty-two.

The environment and climate of Panglau are like Hawai'i. The ocean is like being in Lāhainā. Everything about Panglau resonated within the cells of my body. The customs and traditions are so similar to us Polynesians. The energy that exists here was instantly recognizable to me. The same energy exists in Fiji, Tonga, Samoa, and Hawai'i. It is a kind of energy that is built into the culture and people themselves, a culture of respect for the elders and nature.

When the Tahitians did cross-oceanic voyages, they brought *niu*, coconut, for hydration; *'ulu*, breadfruit, for carbohydrates; and *noni* for medicine. Those three are critically important. The *ninu* (Visaian for *noni*) here is smaller and more potent than *noni* in Hawai'i. I have been reintroducing *noni* in Panglau as a supplement to enhance the immune system. The root, the bark, the stem, the flowers, and the juice all have medicinal value. The flowers can be cooked, the leaves can be used in making tea, and the fruit can be fermented to make *noni* juice.

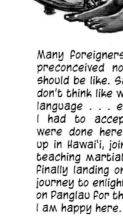

Many foreigners come to these islands with preconceived notions of what these places should be like. Saying things like, "these locals don't think like we do." "They speak a different language . . . etc." When I chose this place, I had to accept the cultural ways things were done here. Ultimately, for me, growing up in Hawai'i, joining the army, competing, and teaching martial arts in the US Mainland, and finally landing on Panglau Island, has been my journey to enlightenment. I have made my home on Panglau for the past thirty-three years and I am happy here.

Illustrated Appendix

This illustrated appendix is a tiny and incomplete sampling of assorted Austronesian words, most of which are cognates and some that are not. There are countless more Austronesian places and cognates, each being incredibly significant, found throughout the regions of "Melanesia," Taiwan, "Maritime (Island) Southeast Asia," "Micronesia," "Polynesia," "Mainland Southeast Asia," Madagasikara, and others, far more than this book can cover. For an extensive list of Austronesian cognates, I recommend visiting Robert Blust and Stephen Trussel's "The Austronesian Comparative Dictionary," which can be found online at http://www.trussel2.com/ACD/. It is also important to note that all the Bol-anon (Vul'anun) words contained here are written using this book's unconventional orthography. For further study of the Cebuano and Bol-anon languages, I recommend John U. Wolff's *A Dictionary of Cebuano Visayan.*

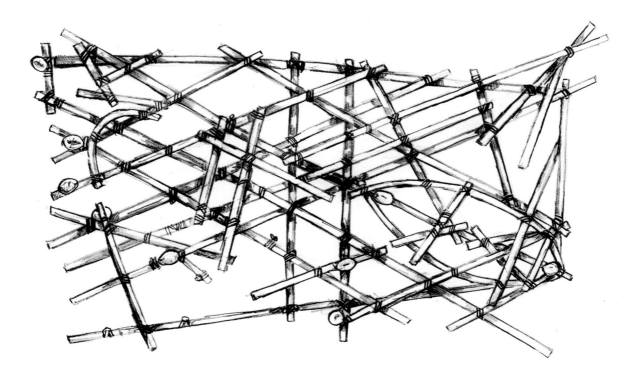

Included Austronesian Languages (Locations)

Anutan (Anuta)
Asilulu (Ambon)
Bahasa Indonesia (Indonesia)
Bahasa Malaysia (Malaysia)
Basa Bali (Bali)
Cebuano (Cebu)
Drehu (Lifou)
Fino' CHamoru (Guåhan)
Gagana Sāmoa (Tutuila)
Ifugao (Luzon)
Ilokano (Luzon)
Itbayaten (Itbayat)
Itneg (Luzon)
Kankanaey (Luzon)

Kiribati (Kiritimati)
Kola (Aru)
Kwênyii (Kunyié / Île des Pins)
Lea Fakatonga (Tonga)
Malagasy (Madagasikara / Madagascar)
Motu (Niugini)
Na Vosa Vakaviti (Viti / Fiji)
'Ōlelo Hawai'i (Hawai'i)
PAN (Proto-Austronesian)
Paumotu (Tuamotu)
PCEMP (Proto-Central-Eastern-Malayo-Polynesian)
POC (Proto-Oceanic)

Puyuma (Taitung County, Taiwan)
Reo Mā'ohi (Taha'a & Tahiti)
Sangir (Sangihe)
Sasak (Lombok)
Sika (Flores)
Tagalog (Luzon)
Te Reo Ipukarea (Rarotonga)
Te Reo Māori (Aotearoa)
Tombo Manggarai (Flores)
Ulithian (Fais)
Vanaŋa Rapa Nui (Rapa Nui)
Vul'anun (Vuhul / Bohol)
Xârâcùù (Grande Terre, Kanaky)
Yami (Ponso no Tao)

	'Ōlelo Hawai'i (Hawai'i)	Kiribati (Kiritimati)	Drehu (Lifou)	Malagasy (Madagasikara)	Vanaŋa Rapa Nui (Rapa Nui)	Reo Mā'ohi (Taha'a & Tahiti)	Gagana Sāmoa (Tutuila)	Vul'anun (Vuhul)
1	kahi	teuana	cas	iray	tahi	ho'e	tasi	usa
2	lua	uoua	lue	roa	rua	piti	lua	duha
3	kolu	tenua	köni	telo	toru	toru	tolu	tulu
4	hā	aua	eke	efatra	hā	maha	fā	upat
5	lima	nimaua	tripi	dimy	rima	pae	lima	līma
6	ono	onoua	cangömen	enina	ōno	ono	ono	unum
7	hiku	itua	luengömen	fito	hitu	hitu	fitu	pītu
8	walu	wanua	köningömen	valo	va'u	va'u	valu	walu
9	iwa	raiwa	ekengömen	sivy	iva	iva	iva	sīam
10	'umi	tebwina	luepi	folo	aŋahuru	'ahuru	sefulu	napūlu

Eye

kârâmè (Grande Terre)
måta (Guåhan)
maka (Hawai'i)
mata (Kiritimati)
maso (Madagasikara)
mata (Rapa Nui)
mata (Taha'a & Tahiti)
mata (Tutuila)
mata (Viti)
mata (Vuhul)

Ear

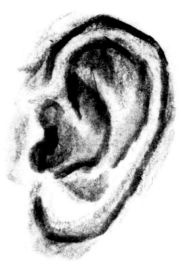

xwânênê (Grande Terre)
pepeiao (Hawai'i)
taninga (Kiritimati)
tainga (Tagalog) (Luzon)
sofina (Madagasikara)
tariŋa (Rapa Nui)
taria (Taha'a & Tahiti)
dunggan (Vuhul)

Nose

kû (Grande Terre)
ihu (Hawai'i)
báiri (Kiritimati)
orona (Madagasikara)
ihu (Rapa Nui)
isu (Tutuila)
ucu (Viti)
īlung (Vuhul)

Hand

mê (Grande Terre)
lima (Hawai'i)
bai (Kiritimati)
tanana (Madagasikara)
rima (Rapa Nui)
rima (Taha'a & Tahiti)
lima (Tutuila)
kāmut (Vuhul)

Mouth / Teeth

nêxwâ / pâ (Grande Terre)
waha / niho (Hawai'i)
wii / wii (Kiritimati)
vava / nify (Madagasikara)
ŋutu / niho (Rapa Nui)
gutu / nifo (Tutuila)
vava / ngīpun (Vuhul)

Navel

piko (Hawai'i)
buto (Kiritimati)
foitrany (Madagasikara)
pito (Rapa Nui)
pūsud (Vuhul)

Above

maluna (Hawai'i)
ambony (Madagasikara)
aruŋa (Rapa Nui)
ini'a (Taha'a & Tahiti)
iluga (Tutuila)
ivāvau (Vuhul)

Below

lalo (Hawai'i)
ambany (Madagasikara)
raro (Rapa Nui)
raro (Taha'a & Tahiti)
lalo (Tutuila)
ilālum (Vuhul)

Mana

mana (Hawai'i: supernatural power or
ability, authority, usually inherited)
mana (Cebu, Vuhul, & Luzon, Tagalog:
inheritance, inherited ability, legacy)
mana (Taha'a & Tahiti: supernatural
power, authority, usually inherited)

Sky

lani (Hawai'i)
kárawa (Kiritimati)
lanitra (Madagasikara)
raŋi (Rapa Nui)
ra'i (Taha'a & Tahiti)
lāngit (Vuhul)

Sun / Day

lā / lā, ao (Hawai'i)
bung / bong (Kiritimati)
araw / araw (Tagalog) (Luzon)
masoandro / andro (Madagasikara)
raá / raá (Rapa Nui)
adlau / adlau (Vuhul)

Moon / Month

mahina / mahina, malama (Hawai'i)
namakáina / namakáina (Kiritimati)
volana / volana (Madagasikara)
mahina / marama (Rapa Nui)
vūlan / vūlan, vūwan (Vuhul)

Rain

ua (Hawai'i)
ua (Taha'a & Tahiti)
uwan (Vuhul)

Red

'ula (Hawai'i)
'ura (archaic) (Taha'a & Tahiti)
pula / puwa (Vuhul)

Land

'āina / honua (Hawai'i)
vanua (Itbayat)
ába (Kiritimati)
tany (Madagasikara)
benua (Malaysia)
kaiŋa / henua (Rapa Nui)
fenua (Taha'a & Tahiti)
vanua (Viti)
iuta / vanua (archaic) (Vuhul)

Rock

pōhaku (Hawai'i)
ati / batano (Kiritimati)
vato (Madagasikara)
ma'ea (Rapa Nui)
vatu (Vuhul)

River

kahawai / muliwai (Hawai'i)
karanga (Kiritimati)
ony / reniraro (Madagasikara)
suva / wāhig (Vuhul)

House / Home

hale / kauhale (Hawai'i)
maeka / kainga (Kiritimati)
trano / fonenana (Madagasikara)
hare (Rapa Nui)
vālai / panimalai (Vuhul)

Mortar (Food Tray) /
Pestle (Food Pounder)

papa ku'i 'ai / pōhaku ku'i 'ai (Hawai'i)
kumete / reru (Rarotonga)
'umete / penu (Taha'a & Tahiti)

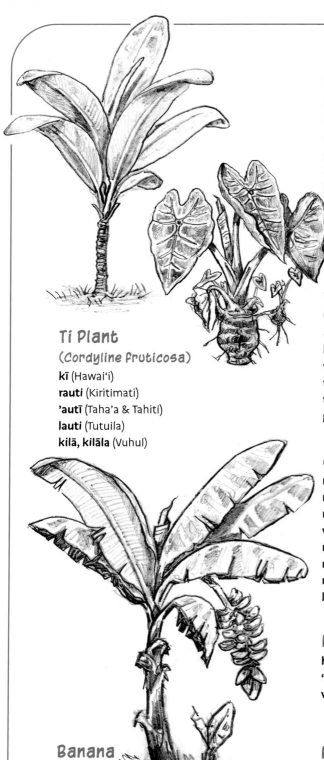

Breadfruit
(Artocarpus altilis)
'ulu (Hawai'i)
mái (Kiritimati)
soanambo (Madagasikara)
'uru (Taha'a & Tahiti)
kulu (Vuhul)

Ti Plant
(Cordyline fruticosa)
kī (Hawai'i)
rauti (Kiritimati)
'autī (Taha'a & Tahiti)
lauti (Tutuila)
kilā, kilāla (Vuhul)

Taro and Giant Taro
(Colocasia esculenta and Alocasia macrorrhizos)
kalo / 'ape (Hawai'i)
viha (Madagasikara)
taro / taro kape (Rapa Nui)
taro / 'ape (Taha'a & Tahiti)
gāvi / pawu / vīga (Vuhul)

Coconut (Cocos nucifera)
niyok (Guåhan)
niu (Hawai'i)
niyog (Tagalog) (Luzon)
vua nihu (Madagasikara)
niu (Rapa Nui)
nū (Rarotonga)
niu (Taha'a & Tahiti)
luvi (Vuhul)

Fruit
hua (Hawai'i)
'ua'ua (Rarotonga)
vunga (Vuhul)

Banana
(Musa)
mai'a (Hawai'i)
funtai, untai (Madagasikara)
maîka (Rapa Nui)
mai'a, mei'a (Taha'a & Tahiti)
sāging (Vuhul)

Hibiscus
(Malvaceae)
aloalo, hau (Hawai'i)
kiaiai (Kiritimati)
varu (Madagasikara)
'aute, pūrau, fau, hau (Taha'a & Tahiti)
gumamela, valintawak (Vuhul)

Flower
pua (Hawai'i)
vūak (Vuhul)

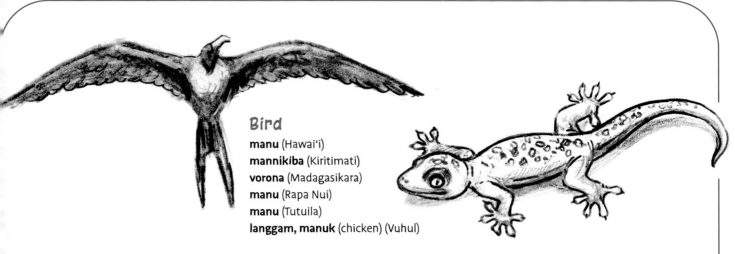

Bird

manu (Hawaiʻi)
mannikiba (Kiritimati)
vorona (Madagasikara)
manu (Rapa Nui)
manu (Tutuila)
langgam, manuk (chicken) (Vuhul)

Gecko, Lizard

moʻo (Hawaiʻi)
beru (Kiritimati)
androngo (Madagasikara)
moʻo (Tutuila)
tikī, tukū (Vuhul)

Sea Turtle

honu (Hawaiʻi)
on (Kiritimati)
fano (Madagasikara)
hônu (Rapa Nui)
iʻa sa (Tutuila)
pawīkan, vaʻū (turtle) (Vuhul)

Fish

iʻa (Hawaiʻi)
ikan (Indonesia)
ika (Kiritimati)
trondro (Madagasikara)
îka (Rapa Nui)
iʻa (Tutuila)
isda / *ikam (Cebu & Vuhul: archaic;
　　see Pigafetta, 1519)

Shark

manō (Hawaiʻi)
ánoi (Kiritimati)
akio (Madagasikara)
maŋó (Rapa Nui)
magō (Tutuila)
īhu (Vuhul)

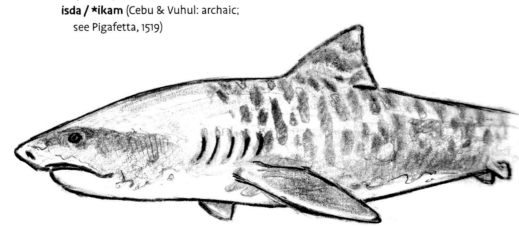

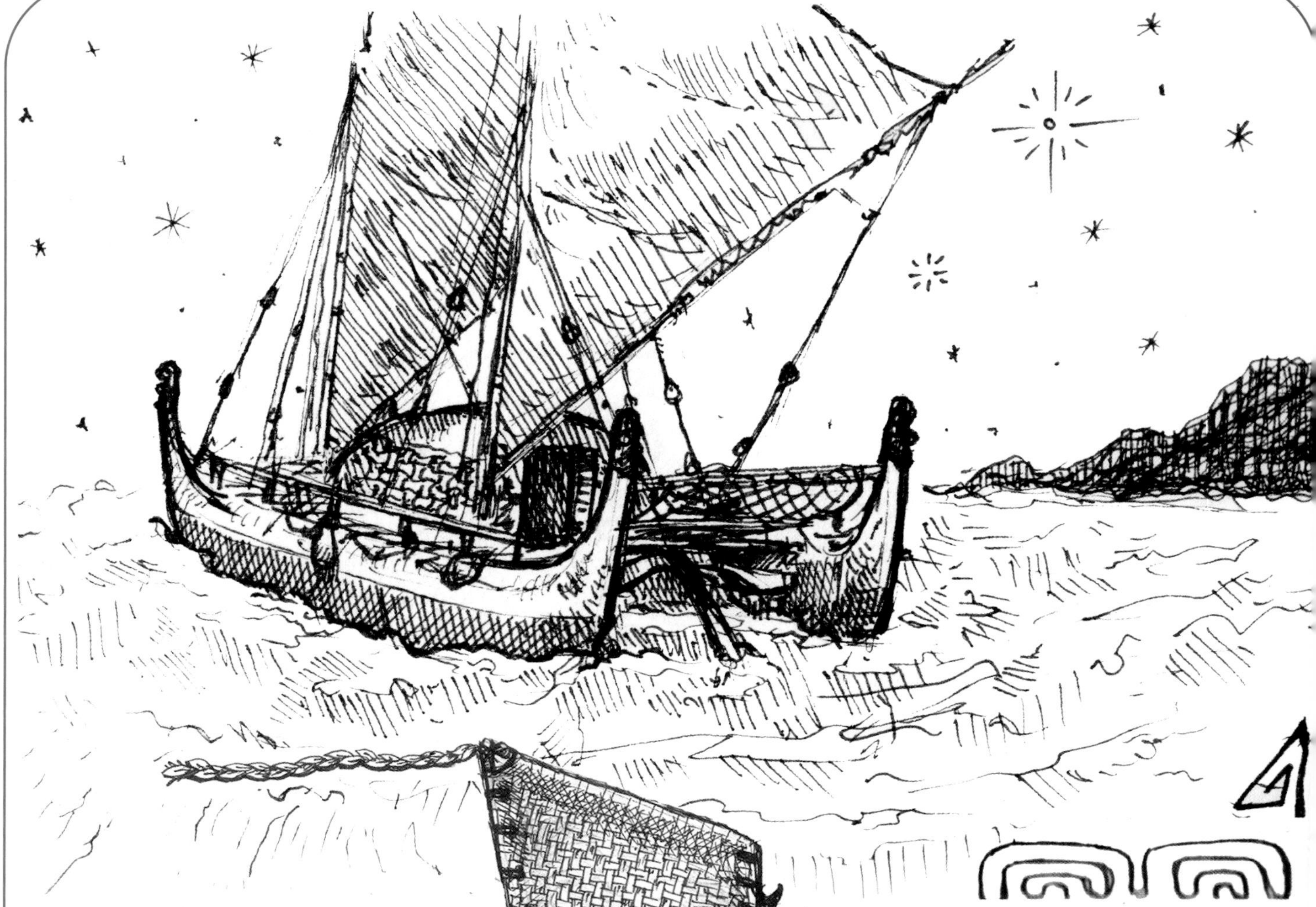

Canoe

*qabaŋ (PAN)
lakana (Madagasikara)
vangka, vanka (Vuhul)
*waŋka (PCEMP)
waŋka (Flores)
*waga (POC)

waka (Aotearoa)
wa‘a (Hawai‘i)
wa (Kiritimati)
vaka (Rarotonga)
va’a (Taha’a & Tahiti)

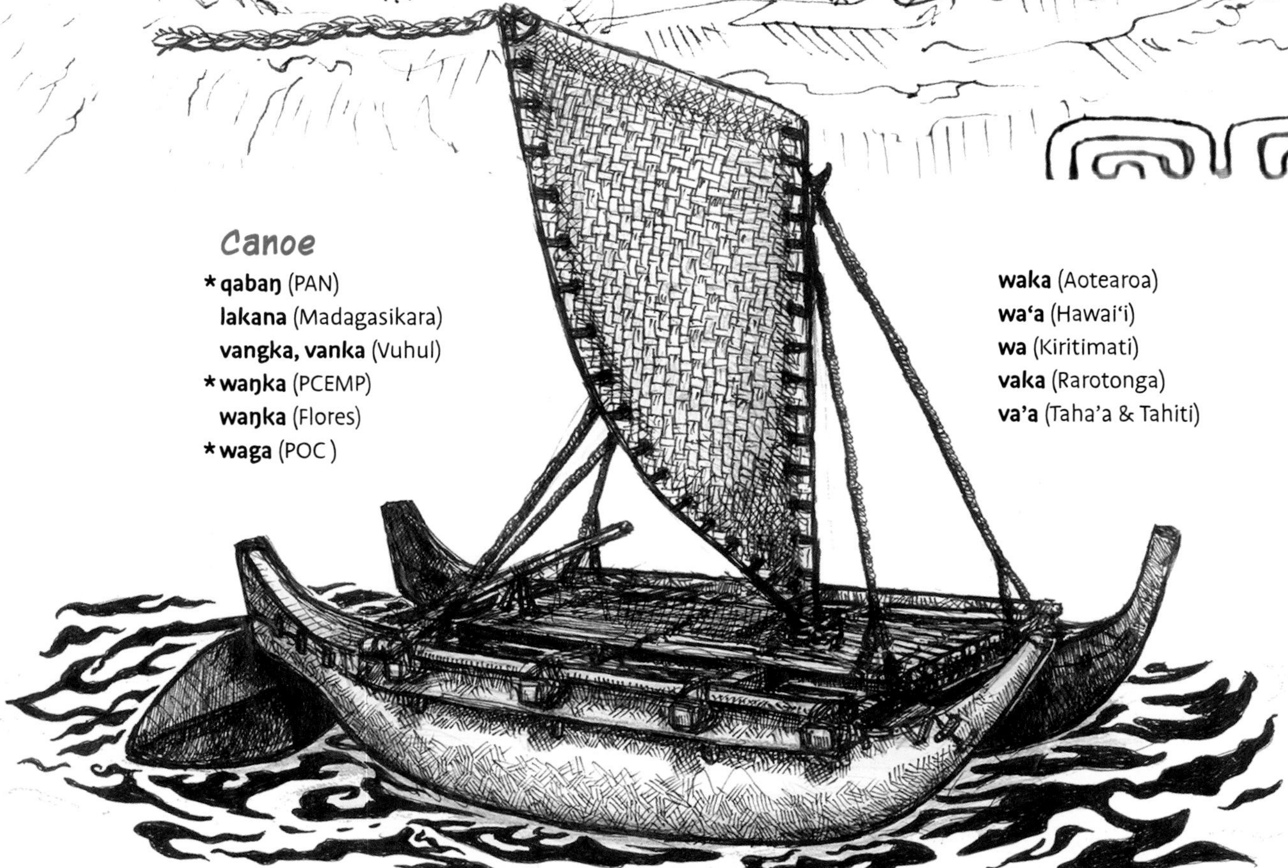

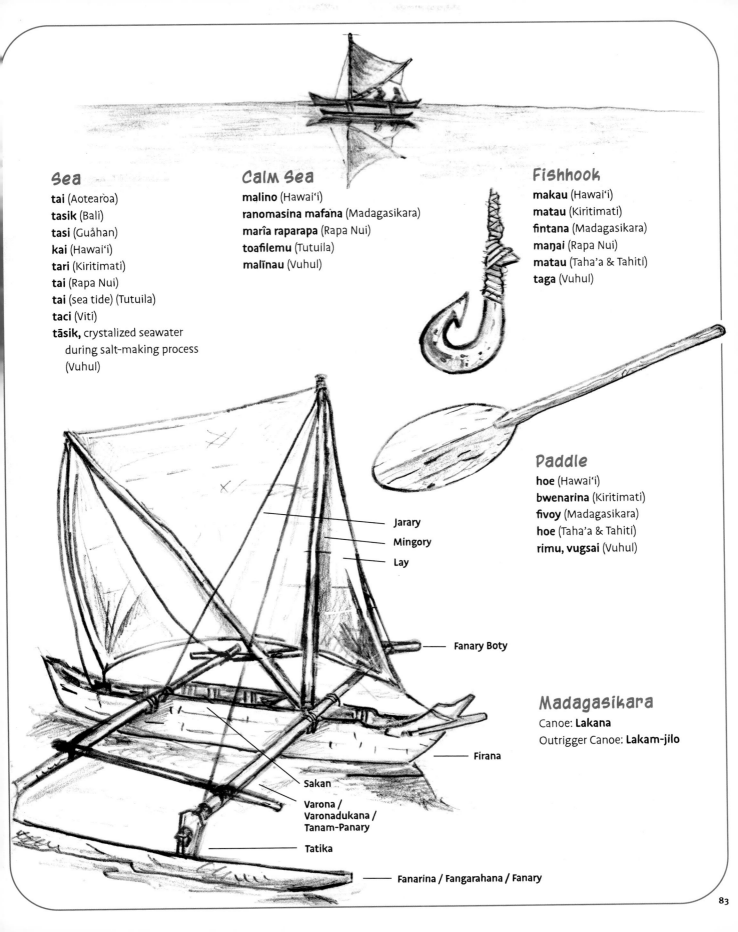

Sea

tai (Aotear̄oa)
tasik (Bali)
tasi (Guåhan)
kai (Hawai'i)
tari (Kiritimati)
tai (Rapa Nui)
tai (sea tide) (Tutuila)
taci (Viti)
tāsik, crystalized seawater
during salt-making process
(Vuhul)

Calm Sea

malino (Hawai'i)
ranomasina mafana (Madagasikara)
marîa raparapa (Rapa Nui)
toafilemu (Tutuila)
malīnau (Vuhul)

Fishhook

makau (Hawai'i)
matau (Kiritimati)
fintana (Madagasikara)
maŋai (Rapa Nui)
matau (Taha'a & Tahiti)
taga (Vuhul)

Paddle

hoe (Hawai'i)
bwenarina (Kiritimati)
fivoy (Madagasikara)
hoe (Taha'a & Tahiti)
rimu, vugsai (Vuhul)

Jarary
Mingory
Lay

Fanary Boty

Madagasikara

Canoe: **Lakana**
Outrigger Canoe: **Lakam-jilo**

Firana

Sakan

Varona /
Varonadukana /
Tanam-Panary

Tatika

Fanarina / Fangarahana / Fanary

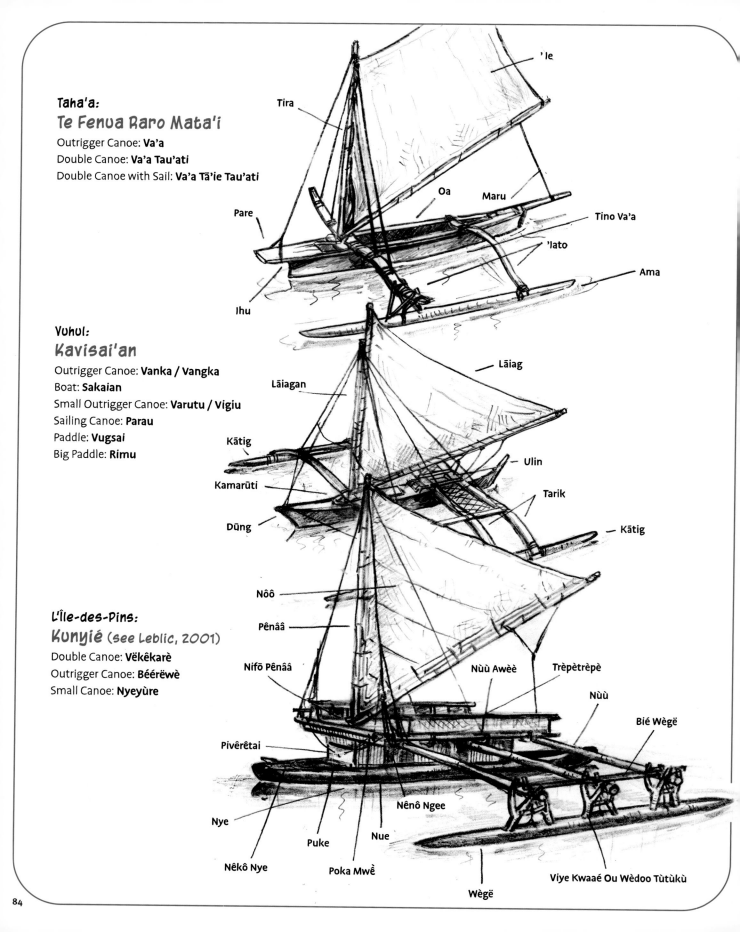

Taha'a:

Te Fenua Raro Mata'i

Outrigger Canoe: **Va'a**
Double Canoe: **Va'a Tau'ati**
Double Canoe with Sail: **Va'a Tā'ie Tau'ati**

'Ie

Tira

Oa

Maru

Pare

Tino Va'a

'Iato

Ama

Ihu

Vuhul:

Kavisai'an

Outrigger Canoe: **Vanka / Vangka**
Boat: **Sakaian**
Small Outrigger Canoe: **Varutu / Vigiu**
Sailing Canoe: **Parau**
Paddle: **Vugsai**
Big Paddle: **Rimu**

Lāiag

Lāiagan

Kātig

Ulin

Kamarūti

Tarik

Dūng

Kātig

Nôô

Pênââ

L'Île-des-Pins:

Kunyié (see Leblic, 2001)

Double Canoe: **Vëkêkarè**
Outrigger Canoe: **Béérëwè**
Small Canoe: **Nyeyùre**

Nifō Pênââ

Nùù Awèè

Trèpètrèpè

Nùù

Bié Wègë

Pivêrêtai

Nênô Ngee

Nye

Puke

Nue

Nêkô Nye

Poka Mwè

Viye Kwaaé Ou Wèdoo Tùtùkù

Wègë

God

akua (Hawai'i)
tuan (lord) (Malaysia)
atua (Rarotonga)
atua (Taha'a & Tahiti)

Gods

Tangaroa (Aotearoa)
Kanaloa (Hawai'i)
Tangaroa (Rarotonga)
Tagaloa (Tutuila)

Lono (Hawai'i)
Rongo (Rarotonga)
Ro'o (Taha'a & Tahiti)

Spirit, Ghost

anti (Kiritimati)
hantu (Malaysia)
aitu (Rarotonga)
aitu (Tutuila)
anītu (Vuhul)

Chief
latu (Ambon)
datu, ratu (Bali)
ratu (Flores)
ratu (Viti)
dātu (Vuhul)

Child
anak (Bali)
kanak kanak (Indonesia)
kanak (Sasak) (Lombok)
anák (Kankanaey) (Luzon)
ánaka (Madagasikara)
kanakán (Ponso no Tao)
alak (Puyuma) (Taitung County, Taiwan)
anāk (Vuhul)

Person
tangata (Aotearoa)
tamata (Aru)
kanaka (Hawai'i)
tau (Motu) (Niugini)
taumata (Sangihe)
taw (Puyuma) (Taitung County, Taiwan)
tagata (Tutuila)
tamata (Viti)
tāwu (Vuhul)

Die
mate (Aotearoa)
mati (Bali)
matai (Guåhan)
make (Hawai'i)
mate (Kiritimati)
máty (Madagasikara)
mate (Tutuila)
matai (Vuhul)

Island
nusa (Bali)
moku, mokupuni, moku'āina (Hawai'i)
ába mákoro (Kiritimati)
nosy (Madagasikara)
motu-motu (Motu) (Niugini)
kaiŋa, motu (Rapa Nui)
pulu (Vuhul)

Māui (Wilcken, 2014)
Motikitiki (Anuta)
Māui Tikitiki (Aotearoa)
Motiktik (Fais)
Māui, Māui Ki'iki'i (Hawai'i)
Nareau Tekitekite (Kiritimati)
Wigan (Ifugao) (Luzon)
Lumauig / Lumawig (Igorot) (Luzon)
Aponitolau (Itneg) (Luzon)
Dumalawi (Itneg) (Luzon)
Māui Ti'iti'i (Taha'a & Tahiti)
Māui Kisikisi (Tonga)
Māui Ti'ti'i, Māui Karukaru (Tuamotu)
Ti'iti'i (Tutuila)
Tubigan (Visaias)

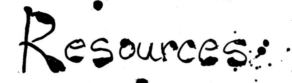

Storytellers

Chantelle from Utah, Tutuila, and Oʻahu
David from Oʻahu and Maui
Francisco from Chile and Rapa Nui
Josia from Madagasikara (Madagascar) and Washington State
Mike from Oʻahu, Maui, and Panglao (Panglau)
Tihoti from Tahaʻa and Tahiti
Tuki from Bohol (Vuhul), Panglao (Panglau), and Oʻahu
Viata from Kiritimati and Tasmania

Linguistic, Cultural, and Academic Advisors

Leah Calunsag from Bohol (Vuhul)
Maria Drake from Bohol (Vuhul)
Tihoti Barff Faara from Tahaʻa and Tahiti
Evangeline Fisher from Bohol (Vuhul)
Tarcisius Kabutaulaka from the University of Hawaiʻi at Mānoa
Marianito Luspo from Holy Name University
Alexander Dale Mawyer from the University of Hawaiʻi at Mānoa
Keao NeSmith from the University of Hawaiʻi at Mānoa
Terence Wesley-Smith from the University of Hawaiʻi at Mānoa

Bibliography

Adelaar, Alexander. 2016. "Austronesians in Madagascar: A Critical Assessment of the Works of Paul Ottino and Philippe Beaujard." In *Early Exchange between Africa and the Wider Indian Ocean World*, edited by Gwyn Campbell, 77–112. London: Palgrave Macmillan.

Ager, Simon. 2020. "Numbers in Rapa Nui (Vananga rapa nui)." https://www.omniglot.com/language/numbers/rapanui.htm.

Aguilar-Pollard, Marlene. 2007. *Myths & Legends of the Philippines: Stories*. Quezon City, Philippines: Jamayco.

Ballard, Chris. 2014. "Oceanic Historicities." *The Contemporary Pacific* 26 (1): 96–124.

Barthel, Thomas S. 1978. *The Eighth Land: The Polynesian Discovery and Settlement of Easter Island*. Honolulu: University Press of Hawai'i.

Be, Zoky. 2013. "Famadihana—Turning the Dead." https://www.madamagazine.com/en/famadihana-die-umbettung-der-toten/.

Beckwith, Martha. 1976. *Hawaiian Mythology*. Honolulu: University Press of Hawai'i.

Bellwood, Peter, James J. Fox, and Darrell T. Tyron. 2006. "The Austronesians in History: Common Origins and Diverse Transformations." In *The Austronesians: Historical and Comparative Perspectives*, edited by Peter Bellwood, James J. Fox, and Darrell T. Tyron, 119–142. Canberra, Australia: ANU E Press.

Bennett, Amanda. 2017, April 5. "When Death Doesn't Mean Goodbye." https://www.nationalgeographic.com/magazine/2016/04/death-dying-grief-funeral-ceremony-corpse/.

Blench, Roger, and Mallam Dendo. 2006. "The Austronesians in Madagascar and on the East African Coast: Surveying the Linguistic Evidence for Domestic and Translocated Animals." Paper presented at Tenth International Conference on Austronesian Linguistics, January 17–20, Puerto Princesa City, Palawan, Philippines.

Brewster, Adolph. 1967. *The Hill Tribes of Fiji*. New York: Johnson Repr. Corp.

Calvert, James, and Thomas Williams. 1860. "Manners and Customs." In *In Fiji and the Fijians*, edited by George Stringer Rowe, 137–138. New York: D. Appleton and Company.

Carroll, Jeffrey, Brandy Nālani McDougall, and Georganne Nordstrom, eds. 2015. *Huihui: Navigating Art and Literature in the Pacific*. Honolulu: University of Hawai'i Press.

The Chamorro Language. 2020, September 12. "Chamorro Words and Common Phrases." http://www.chamoru.info/language-lessons/chamorro-words-common-phrases/.

Conant, Carlos Everett. 1909. "The Names of Philippine Languages." *Anthropos* 4 (4): 1069–1074.

Craig, Robert D. 2004. *Handbook of Polynesian Mythology*. Santa Barbara, CA: ABC-CLIO.

Dening, Greg. 1991. "A Poetic for Histories: Transformations that Present the Past." In *Clio in Oceania: Toward a Historical Anthropology*, edited by Aletta Biersack, 347–381. Washington, DC: Smithsonian Institute Press.

Diaz, Vicente M. 2011. "Voyaging for Anti-Colonial Recovery: Austronesian Seafaring, Archipelagic Rethinking, and the Re-mapping of Indigeneity." *Pacific Asia Inquiry* 2 (1): 21–32.

Dixon, Roland B. 1964. *Oceanic Mythology*. New York: Cooper Square.

Douglas, Bronwen. 2010. "Terra Australis to Oceania." *The Journal of Pacific History* 45 (2): 179–210. Abingdon, UK: Taylor and Francis, Ltd.

Dunis, Serge. 2009. *Pacific Mythology, Thy Name Is Woman: From Asia to the Americas in the Quest for the Island of Women: How the Neolithic Canoes Left Behind an Epic Wake*. Papeete, Tahiti, French Polynesia: Haere Po.

Durocher, Christian. 2003, April 2. "'Haka Pei': Easter Island's Test of Courage." http://www.pireport.org/articles/2003/04/02/haka-pei-easter-island's-test-courage.

Eiseman, Fred B., Jr. 1996. *Bali: Sekala and Niskala: Essays on Religion, Ritual, and Art*. Berkeley, CA: Periplus Editions.

Fanon, Frantz. 1968. *The Wretched of the Earth*. New York: Grove Press.

Finney, Ben. 2007. "Ocean Sailing Canoes." In *Vaka Moana: Voyages of the Ancestors: The Discovery and Settlement of the Pacific*, edited by K. R. Howe, 102–153. Honolulu: University of Hawai'i Press.

Flao, Benjamin. 2014. *Vaa: Une Saison aux Tuamotu*. Paris: Futuropolis.

Flood, Bo, Beret Strong, and William Flood. 1999. *Pacific Island Legends: Tales from Micronesia, Melanesia, Polynesia, and Australia*. Honolulu: Bess Press.

Frazier, Sir James George. 1996. *The Golden Bough: A Study of Magic and Religion*. London: Penguin Books.

Garden, Donald, and Mark R. Stoll. 2005. *Australia, New Zealand, and the Pacific: An Environmental History*. Santa Barbara, CA: ABC-CLIO.

Gatty, Ronald. 2009. *Fijian-English Dictionary with Notes on Fijian Culture and Natural History*. Suva, Fiji: Gatty.

Gegeo, David Welchman. 2001. "(Re)visioning Knowledge Transformation in the Pacific: A Response to Subramani's 'The Oceanic Imaginary.'" *The Contemporary Pacific* 13 (1): 178–183.

Giambelli, Rodolpho A. 2001. "The Coconut, the Body and the Human Being. Metaphors of Life and Growth in Nusa

Penida and Bali." In *The Social Life of Trees: Anthropological Perspectives on Tree Symbolism*, edited by Laura M. Rival, 133–152. Oxford: Berg.

Gibbons, Ann. 2016, October 3. " 'Game-changing' Study Suggests First Polynesians Voyaged All the Way from East Asia." http://www.sciencemag.org/news/2016/10/game-changing-study-suggests-first-polynesians-voyaged-all-way-east-asia.

Griffith, Marie. 2013, May 2. "Legend of Coconut Tree (Hina and the Eel King)—Tahiti." http://folklore.usc.edu/?p=18636.

Guppy, Henry B. 1866, January 1. "The Polynesians and Their Plant-Names." *Journal of the Transactions of the Victoria Institute, or Philosophical Society of Great Britain.* Victoria Institute (Great Britain). https://archive.org/details/journaloftransac291897vict/page/n7.

Handy, E. S. Craighill. 1923. *The Native Culture in the Marquesas.* Honolulu: The Bishop Museum.

Hanlon, David. 2017. "Losing Oceania to the Pacific and the World." *The Contemporary Pacific* 29 (2): 286–318.

Hau'ofa, Epeli. 1994. "Our Sea of Islands." *The Contemporary Pacific* 6 (1): 147–161.

———. 2007. *Tales of the Tikongs.* Honolulu: University of Hawai'i Press.

———. 2008. "Pasts to Remember." In *We Are the Ocean: Selected Works,* by Epeli Hau'ofa, 100–119. Honolulu: University of Hawai'i Press.

———. 2008b. "The Ocean in Us." In *We Are the Ocean: Selected Works,* by Epeli Hau'ofa, 41–59. Honolulu: University of Hawai'i Press.

Hereniko, Vilsoni. 1995. *Woven Gods: Female Clowns and Power in Rotuma.* Honolulu: University of Hawai'i Press.

———. 2000. "Indigenous Knowledge and Academic Imperialism." In *Remembrance of Pacific Pasts: An Invitation to Remake History,* edited by Robert Borofsky, 78–91. Honolulu: University of Hawai'i Press.

Hornell, James. 1920. "The Common Origin of the Outrigger Canoes of Madagascar and East Africa." *Man* 20:134–139.

Irwin, Geoffrey. 2007. "Voyaging and Settlement." In *Vaka Moana: Voyages of the Ancestors: The Discovery and Settlement of the Pacific,* edited by K. R. Howe, 56–91. Honolulu: University of Hawai'i Press.

Jenkins, David A. 2008. "A Day of Research on Pamilácan Island: A Mini-Travelogue." *Philippine Quarterly of Culture and Society* 36 (1/2): 27–37.

Jolly, Margaret. 2007. "Imagining Oceania: Indigenous and Foreign Representations of a Sea of Islands." *The Contemporary Pacific* 19 (2): 508–545.

Jones, Neville. 1912. "The Story of Ifaramalemy and Ikotobekibo." *Man* 12:125–127.

Kabutaulaka, Tarcisius. 2015. "Re-Presenting Melanesia: Ignoble Savages and Melanesian Alter-Natives." *The Contemporary Pacific* 27 (1): 110–146.

Kauvaka, Lea Lani Kinikini. 2016. "Berths and Anchorages: Pacific Cultural Studies from Oceania." *The Contemporary Pacific* 28 (1): 130–151.

King, Thomas. 2011. *The Truth About Stories.* New York: House of Anansi Press.

Kirch, Patrick Vinton. 2017. *On the Road of the Winds: An Archaeological History of the Pacific Islands before European Contact.* Berkeley: University of California Press.

Kun, Ho Chuan. 2007. On the Origins of Taiwanese Austronesians. In *Vaka Moana: Voyages of the Ancestors: The Discovery and Settlement of the Pacific,* edited by K. R. Howe, 92–93. Honolulu: University of Hawai'i Press.

Lawler, Andrew. 2017, December 9. "Ancient Crop Remains Record Epic Migration to Madagascar." http://www.sciencemag.org/news/2016/05/ancient-crop-remains-record-epic-migration-madagascar.

Leblic, Isabelle. 2001. "Une Pirogue Pontée à L'île des Pins (Nouvelle-Calédonie)." *Techniques & Culture* 35–36:1–20. doi: 10.4000/tc.296.

Litogo. 2007. *Binisaya! | Ato ni Bay!* https://www.binisaya.com.

Loarca, Miguel de. (1582) 1903. "Relacion de las Yslas Filipinas por Miguel de Loarca." In *The Philippine Islands, 1493–1803: Volume V, 1582–1583,* edited by Emma Helen Blair and James Alexander Robertson, 29–81. Cleveland: The Arthur H. Clark Company. https://www.gutenberg.org/files/16501/16501-h/16501-h.htm#d0e420.

Martratt, Joyce. 2007, August 21. "Ask Joyce: What's the Legend about Guam's First Coconut Tree." https://www.andersen.af.mil/News/Commentaries/Display/Article/416927/ask-joyce-whats-the-legend-about-guams-first-coconut-tree/.

Mila, Karlo. 2005. *Dream Fish Floating.* Wellington, Aotearoa New Zealand: Huia.

Mita, Merata. 1993. "Indigenous Literature in a Colonial Society." In *Te Ao Marama: Regaining Aotearoa: Maori Writers Speak Out,* vol. 2, edited by Witi Ihimaera, 310–314. Auckland, Aotearoa New Zealand: Reed Books.

Moorefield, John C. 2020. *Māori Dictionary.* https://maoridictionary.co.nz/.

Morse, Janice. 1992. "Childbirth in Fiji." In *Cross-Cultural Nursing: Anthropological Approaches to Nursing Research,* 44–45. Philadelphia: Gordon and Breach Science Publishers.

Moyse-Faurie, Claire, et al. 2011, October 19. "Body Parts in Xârâcùù." https://www.youtube.com/watch?v=LiIxuf4ZXkM.

Mulloy, Brigid. 2016, November. "Banana Sleds & Body Paint." https://hanahou.com/19.5/banana-sleds-body-paint.

Munnik, Joe, and Katy Scott. 2017, March 28. "Famadihana: The Family Reunion Where the Dead Get an Invite." https://edition.cnn.com/2016/10/18/travel/madagascar-turning-bones/index.html.

National Park of American Samoa. 2015. "The Samoan Creation Legend." https://www.nps.gov/npsa/learn/historyculture/legendpo.htm.

Odango, Emerson L. 2015. "Austronesian Youth Perspectives on Language Reclamation and Maintenance." *The Contemporary Pacific* 27 (1): 73–108.

Osorio, Jonathan K. 2004. "Gazing Back: Communing with Our Ancestors." *Educational Perspectives* 37 (1): 14–17.

Otsuka, Yuko. 2007. "Making a Case for Tongan as an Endangered Language." *The Contemporary Pacific* 19 (2): 446–473.

Pajo, Maria Caseñas. 1954. "Bohol Folklore." Master's thesis, University of San Carlos.

Penny, David, and Anna Meyer. 2007. "DNA and the Settlement of Polynesia." In *Vaka Moana: Voyages of the Ancestors: The Discovery and Settlement of the Pacific,* edited by K. R. Howe, 98–99. Honolulu: University of Hawai'i Press.

Pigafetta, Antonio. (1519) 1906. *The Philippine Islands, 1493–1898: Volume XXXIII, 1519–1522,* edited by Emma Helen Blair and James Alexander Robertson. Cleveland: The Arthur H. Clark Company. https://www.gutenberg.org/files/42884/42884-h/42884-h.htm.

Pukui, Mary Kawena. 1983. *'Ōlelo No'eau: Hawaiian Proverbs and Poetical Sayings.* Honolulu: Bishop Museum Press.

Pulang Lupa Foundation. "Tungkod-pare." http://www.stuartxchange.org/TungkodPare.html.

Rehg, Kenneth L. 2004. "Linguists, Literacy, and the Law of Unintended Consequences." *Oceanic Linguistics* 43 (2): 498–518.

Ruud, Jorgen. 1970. *Taboo: A Study of Malagasy Customs and Beliefs.* Oslo: Oslo University Press.

Ryle, Jacqueline. 2017. "Paths Across Space and Time." In *My God, My Land: Interwoven Paths of Christianity and Tradition in Fiji.* London: Routledge.

Sablan, Jerick. 2017, March 3. "Residents Challenged to Speak Only Chamorro on Sunday." https://www.guampdn.com/story/news/2017/03/03/residents-challenged-speak-only-chamorro-sunday/98671108/.

Said, Edward. 1978. *Orientalism.* New York: Pantheon Books.

Şengör, A. M. Celâl, et al. 2019, October 18. "Asia." https://www.britannica.com/place/Asia/Geologic-history

Sieber, Claudio. 2017, October 13. "Living with Corpses: How Indonesia's Toraja People Deal with the Dead." https://www.scmp.com/magazines/post-magazine/long-reads/article/2115027/living-corpses-how-indonesias-toraja-people-deal.

Skoglund, Peter, et al. 2016. "Genomic Insights into the Peopling of the Southwest Pacific." *Nature* 538:510–513. https://doi.org/10.1038/nature19844.

Smith, Linda Tuhiwai. 1999. *Decolonizing Methodologies: Research and Indigenous Peoples.* Dunedin, Aotearoa New Zealand: University of Otago Press.

Spaelti, Philip. 2015. "Rongorongo." http://kohaumotu.org/Rongorongo/index.html

Sparks, Emily. 2000. "Compliance and Care: An Ethnography of a Fijian Village." Thesis, Union College, NY.

Spitz, Chantal T. 2007. *Island of Shattered Dreams.* Wellington, Aotearoa New Zealand: Huia Publishers.

Spriggs, Matthew. 2006. "The Lapita Culture and Austronesian Prehistory in Oceania." In *The Austronesians: Historical and Comparative Perspectives,* edited by Peter Bellwood, James J. Fox, and Darrell T. Tryon, 119–142. Canberra: ANU E Press.

———. 2009. "Oceanic Currents in Deep Time." *Pacificurrents* 1 (1): 7–27.

Stead, Victoria C. 2017. *Becoming Landowners: Entanglements of Custom and Modernity in Papua New Guinea and Timor-Leste.* Honolulu: University of Hawai'i Press.

Subramani. 2001. The Oceanic Imaginary. *The Contemporary Pacific* 13 (1): 149–162.

Te Ipukarea, and University of the South Pacific. 2020. "Dictionary of Cook Islands Languages." http://cookislandsdictionary.com/.

Te Papa Tongarewa. 2006. "Whenua to Whenua." https://collections.tepapa.govt.nz/topic/1437.

Teaiwa, Teresia. 1995. "Scholarship from a Lazy Native." In *Work in Flux,* edited by Emma Greenwood, Klaus Neuman, and Andrew Sartori, 58–72. Parkville, Victoria, Australia: University of Melbourne History Department.

———. 2011. "Preparation for Deep Learning." *The Journal of Pacific History* 46 (2): 214–220.

Tengan, Ty P. Kāwika. 2005. "Unsettling Ethnography: Tales of an 'Oiwi in the Anthropological Slot." *Anthropological Forum* 15 (3): 247–256.

Thaman, Konai Helu. 2003. "Decolonizing Pacific Studies: Indigenous Perspectives, Knowledge, and Wisdom in Higher Education." *The Contemporary Pacific* 15 (1): 1–17.

Tikao, Kelly. 2012. "Iho: A Cord Between Two Worlds." Thesis, Centre for Science Communication, University of Otago, Aotearoa New Zealand.

Trask, Haunani K. 1999. *From a Native Daughter: Colonialism and Sovereignty in Hawai'i.* Honolulu: University of Hawai'i Press.

Trussel, Stephen. 2003. "Kiribati—English Finderlist." https://www.trussel.com/kir/dic/find_a.htm.

Trussel, Stephen, and Robert Blust. 2017. "Austronesian Comparative Dictionary." http://www.trussel2.com/ACD/.

Tsukamoto, Katsumi, and Mari Kuroki. 2014. *Eels and Humans*. Tokyo: Springer Japan.

Tupara, Hope. 2011, May 5. "Te Whānau Tamariki—Pregnancy and Birth—Rites and Baby Care." www.teara.govt.nz.

Wendt, Albert. 1983. "Towards a New Oceania." In *A Pacific Islands Collection: Seaweeds and Constructions*, edited by Richard Hamasaki, no. 7: 71–85.

Wesley-Smith, Terence. 1995. "Rethinking Pacific Islands Studies." *Pacific Studies* 18 (2): 115–137.

———. 2016. "Rethinking Pacific Studies Twenty Years On." *The Contemporary Pacific* 28 (1): 153–169.

White, Geoffrey M., and Ty Kāwika Tengan. 2001. "Disappearing Worlds: Anthropology and Cultural Studies in Hawai'i and the Pacific." Special issue, *The Contemporary Pacific* 13 (2): 381–416.

Wilcken, Lane. 2014. *The Forgotten Children of Maui: Filipino Myths, Tattoos, and Rituals of a Demigod*. San Bernardino, CA: Createspace.

Winduo, Steven. 2000. "Unwriting Oceania: The Repositioning of the Pacific Writer Scholars within a Folk Narrative Space." *New Literary History* 31 (3): 599–613.

Wolff, John. 1972. *A Dictionary of Cebuano Visayan*. Ithaca, NY: Cornell University, Southeast Asia Program and Linguistic Society of the Philippines.

Wood, Houston. 2003. "Cultural Studies for Oceania." *The Contemporary Pacific* 15 (2): 340–374.

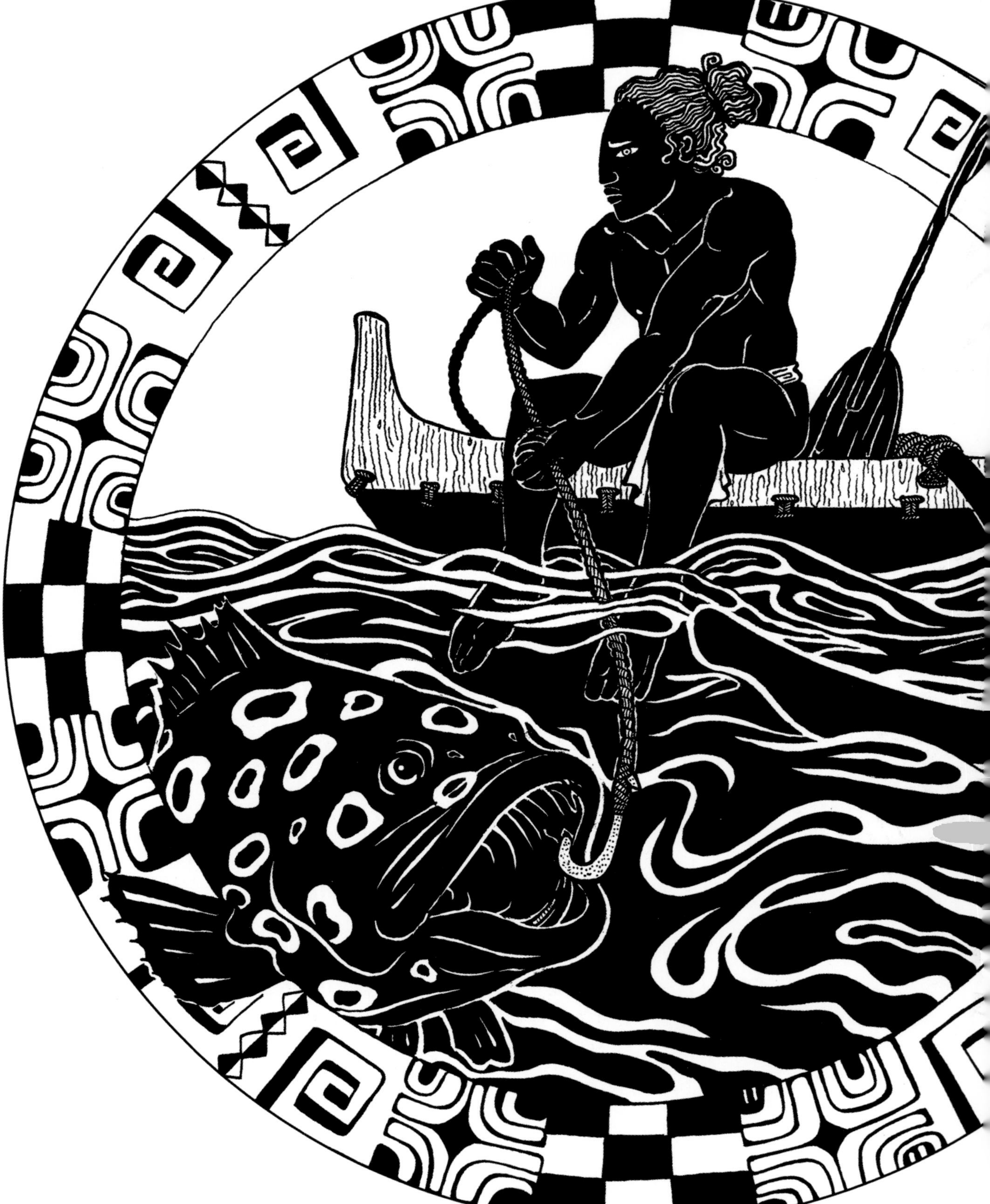

Aaron Daniel Motuki Herefenua Drake, who simply goes by Tuki or Fenua, was born on Vuhul (Bohol) in the Visaias (Visayas) Islands and spent much of his life traveling across the Pacific Ocean. He is of Austronesian, European, East Asian, and Melanesian heritage.

Drake has always had a profound attachment to the Pacific and is passionate about Austronesian cultures, histories, oral traditions, languages, art, tattoos, migration, and voyaging. He calls the islands of Hawai'i and the Visaias (Visayas) home and has been married for more than ten years to his wife, Ashley, with whom he shares two incredible children.

Drake strives to be a lifelong learner with a humble heart and an open mind. He earned his MA degree in 2018 from the Center for Pacific Islands Studies at the University of Hawai'i at Mānoa where he also received the Foreign Language Acquisition Scholarship and the mark of distinction on his MA Comprehensive Examination. He graduated Summa Cum Laude from Brigham Young University–Hawai'i with a BA in Pacific Island Studies in 2017 and an AA in Hawaiian Studies in 2015 from Kaua'i Community College where he was involved with the voyaging group, Nā Kālai Wa'a O Kaua'i.

Currently, Drake is director of operations for a nonprofit foundation that supports the Deaf community in the Visaias (Visayas) Islands and the founder of Kinabuhi Farm, a nonprofit organic farm. He was formerly a project coordinator, an illustrator, and a taro farmer; he also interned with the Cook Islands Ministry of Culture and worked as a high school art teacher.

Through storytelling, art, and education, Drake hopes to inspire and empower the next generation of Austronesians. He wants to encourage them to explore their interwoven pasts, restore old connections fragmented by Western colonization, and develop new interoceanic relationships with their fellow Austronesian coheirs.